Knowing Jesus
Our Lord, Our Servant

Bill Syrios

Cook Communications

Victor is an imprint of
Cook Communications Ministries, Colorado Springs, Colorado 80918
Cook Communications, Paris, Ontario
Kingsway Communications, Eastbourne, England

Editor: Carolyn Nystrom
Cover Design: Scott Rattray
Cover Photo: Nick Vedros

Recommended Dewey Decimal Classification: 226.1
Suggested Subject Heading: NT, GOSPELS
ISBN: 1-56476-350-1

5 6 7 8 9 10 11 12 Printing/Year 07 06 05 04 03 02 01 00

Contents

Welcome to TruthSeed

I am a planter. Each spring finds me stooped in my garden, loose dirt churned soft by winter storms oozing into my worn sneakers, the smell of compost twitching my nose, warm sun thawing the muscles of my back, and precious seed—radish, carrots, lettuce, peas, beans, corn, beets, watermelon, cantaloupe, squash, cosmos, marigold, zinnia—trickling through my fingers. It's my favorite phase of gardening, one I try to remember as I tug at thick weeds in late June's humidity, swat mosquitoes in sweltering July twilight, and heft baskets of produce into my August-cluttered kitchen. I cut, peel, blanch, can, freeze, and (in recent years) mostly give away—with neighbors and coworkers cashing in on my penchant for planting. It's hard to believe that seeds barely filling a lunch bag spend a few weeks blending God's creative magic of sun, soil, and water into a winter's worth of food for a family. But that's what seed is all about. Abundant life encased in a tiny, hard shell.

No mere book can deliver full-grown, harvested produce—though some come close. Like seeds, books contain a grain of truth encased in the crusty shell of words. But plant that seed in the right season in a mind ready to learn, tug out the weeds of distraction that disrupt study, water it with a sweated-out attempt to put its truths into practice, invite with prayer the sunshine of God's grace, and expect a crop—enough to nurture personal growth, enough to give away.

What harvest can we expect from TruthSeed?

We can expect to know Scripture. Each book in this series invites us to explore either a topic addressed in several biblical passages or to study an entire book of the Bible. These are inductive studies. Each session leads us to explore a single passage on three levels: details of information presented in the text, accurate interpretation of that information, and personal response.

We can expect to experience God's presence. Scripture points us to God, its author and its object. It is His letter to us about Himself. As we read, study, and meditate on Scripture we will become more and more aware of God. We will see His love and wrath, His mercy and justice, acted out on the pages of these ancient texts. And we will know more and more about God's personal care for us and His desire for us to respond to Him.

We can expect to improve our relationships. Human nature is remarkably resilient; over the millenniums we have changed little. Scripture shows us brothers who hate each other enough to kill, and friends who love each other more than their own lives. It shows us the grief of death and the joy of birth. It shows us the celebration of marriage and the pain of marriage ended. It pictures overwhelming generosity and the grudging hunger of greed. It echoes our hopeless moans at life's futility and it shouts our hope for life beyond this life. As Scripture increases our understanding of each other, we can expect to see its fruit wherever we touch other people: at work, in friendships, at churches, in neighborhoods, in casual encounters with waitresses and store clerks, and in the most challenging of all relationships: our families.

We can expect to better understand ourselves. Scripture is an intensely personal book. True, we may read it for historical content, or for its quality literature, or for its insightful teachings. But if Scripture is to accomplish its true purpose, we must read its pages, open ourselves, and allow it to read our souls. Scripture will show us our faults: the jealous brother, the greedy servant, the pompous keeper of laws. But as we let Scripture do its work, we will grow more and more according to God's design: the forgiving parent, the faithful leader, the wise friend, the one who models the love of Jesus Christ. And we will find the empty, God-shaped hole inside being filled by Christ Himself. Even people who don't believe much of what the Bible says, who are turned off by sermons and essays, can appreciate the questions here that allow them to examine the biblical text for themselves, explore its potential meanings, and form personal conclusions about response.

TruthSeed is appropriate for small group discussion or for personal use. Its blend of academic, personal, and relational tasks make it ideal for cell groups, workplace study groups, neighborhood groups, school-based groups, Sunday School classes, retreats, and outreach groups. It is also for personal study, meditation, and growth.

Suggestions for Group Discussion

1. There's no need to be a Bible expert to participate in a TruthSeed discussion. You may find experts in your group, but there is plenty of room for non-experts as well. Since the discussion centers around a single passage, you will all participate on a similar level. And God can grow any of us.

2. Arrive on time — out of consideration for other group members. Bring your TruthSeed guide and a Bible.

3. Commit to regular attendance. Understanding of the Scripture and relationships within the group are cumulative. You and others will benefit most if you can count on each other to be there. If you must be absent, call your host or leader ahead of time.

4. Discussion is a shared responsibility. It blends talking and listening in even balance. If you are a born listener, act on your responsibility to share your insights by making the extra effort necessary. If you are a born talker, sharpen your listening skills by keeping track of the flow of conversation. If you discover that you are "on stage" more than the average person present, shorten your comments and use them to draw other people into the conversation.

5. Treat other group members with respect. You cannot possibly agree with every comment throughout the course of a discussion study. Disagreement is one way to help each other grow toward the truth. But express your disagreement in kind terms that reflect a genuine respect for the person.

6. Guard the privacy of people in your group. Since spiritual growth makes a deep impact on our personal lives, you will likely hear others speak of their private feelings and events. And you may want to speak some of your own private thoughts. Agree together that you will not divulge each other's stories.

7. Don't gossip. Many groups pray together for a variety of needy people. It's tempting to get specific about names and weaknesses in a way that invites more speculation than prayer. Don't do it. It's possible to pray for a person with very little inside information. God knows it anyway.

8. Be willing to discuss the application questions. Some people are content to keep a group study at a purely academic level, so they read the questions that invite personal response, and pass on with the quick instruction to "think about it." But if Scripture is to be more than a textbook of information, we must allow it to penetrate our lives. Members of a group can nurture each other toward spiritual growth as they discuss together its personal impact.

9. Take note of the follow-up assignments. Each TruthSeed study ends with supplementary material that can provide further enrichment. In some cases, this section may prove as valuable as the rest of the study. So take advantage of this added resource.

10. Consider leading a discussion. Many groups rotate leadership so that almost everyone takes a turn asking the questions. This job does not require a lot of special skills, but a few pointers won't hurt. If it's your turn to lead, you will find notes for leaders beginning on page 77.

Suggestions for Personal Study

1. Settle into your favorite "quiet time" spot. Bring your Bible, the TruthSeed guide, writing materials, and (if you like) a commentary or Bible dictionary.

2. Pray. Ask God to reveal Himself to you as you study. Ask that He assist your understanding, that He bare your inner self to His gaze, and that He use your time to bring healing to your relationships.

3. Begin by reading the chapter introduction. Make notes about the first question and allow it to help you approach the topic you are about to study.

4. Read the assigned biblical text. If textual accuracy is one of your priorities, use a contemporary translation (not a paraphrase) that reflects recent scholarship. Mark significant words or phrases in your Bible, draw lines between ideas that seem connected, write questions or comments in the margins. Try reading aloud. It's one of the best ways to keep your mind from wandering.

5. Work through the list of questions. Jot notes in the space provided. Keep a journal of answers that require more space or more lengthy personal reflection.

6. Stop for periods of silence and meditation throughout your quiet time to allow God to work in your inner being.

7. Continue to pray as you study, asking God to reveal what He wants you to know of yourself and of Himself. Read aloud sections of the passage as a prayer inserting "I" and "me" where appropriate—or insert the name of someone you care about.

8. Don't feel that you must do an entire lesson at a single sitting. Feel free to break at natural division points or whenever you have "had enough" for now. Then come back on a different day, reread the text, review your work thus far, and pick up where you left off.

9. When you have completed your personal study of the questions, turn to the appropriate leader's notes in the back of the guide to gain further information you may have missed. If you are the studious type, refer to a commentary or Bible dictionary for more insights. The reading list at the end of the book provides a list of reliable resources.

10. Put the follow-up activities at the end of each study into practice. Read, sing, pray, do, meditate, journal, make the phone call, start the project, repair the relationship. When your study time is finished, God's work in your life has just begun. Allow His work to continue throughout the week.

As you use this TruthSeed guide, I pray that seeds of truth from God's Word will grow a rich harvest in your life.

—Carolyn Nystrom, Editor

Introducing Knowing Jesus

Maybe I should have considered other options. Maybe my interest in the New Testament disciples of Jesus would be thought excessive. Maybe, just maybe, I was trying to live out a fantasy of what it was like to be an early follower of Jesus.

One way or another, my wife Teresa and I ended up with four boys named Luke, Andrew, Phillip, and Mark. If I had had all the say, it might just be: Matthew, Mark, Luke and John. Fortunately, Teresa exercised some common sense.

Of course, considering their namesakes, we could have done a lot worse. The four men whose names are associated with these New Testament accounts have bequeathed to us a record of inestimable worth. Their unique message becomes stereophonic or, more accurately, quadraphonic as these authors describe similar events from four different vantage points. It's like listening to four witnesses whose testimonies add increasing dimension and credibility to the others. Their own unlikely fame derives from their most unusual subject.

Few if any would have predicted the impact made on history by Nazareth's most famous native son. Upon leaving His life as a carpenter, He lived only three years as a preacher and healer. Though He never wrote anything, more has been written about Him than any other individual in history. Though He never initiated political change, His teachings have produced profound societal transformation. Whatever you know or believe about Jesus of Nazareth, His impact on history is inescapable.

Like the man Himself, the accounts of Jesus' life and ministry are unique in the field of literature. Ancient writings include historical accounts, personal memoirs, mythological stories, and biographies. But none of these styles describe the genre in which Matthew, Mark, Luke, and John wrote. As authors they combine the roles of historian, biographer, theologian, and pastor. The authors do not report events as neutral observers but as men who have been deeply influenced by the message they desire to communicate. Lacking literary precedent, second-century Christians called these authors *Evangelists* and their record *The Gospels.*

The English word "gospel" comes from a Greek word which means "good news." Of course the Gospel writers' enthusiasm does not focus on just any joyful report but on the word from God that He has come into the world as a human being. And if this isn't remarkable enough, this God-Human came with all the fanfare of birth to a humble Jewish family in a rented barn. In this act and the ones to follow, Jesus increasingly clarified just what His purpose was. Many Jewish people were expecting a Messiah who would vanquish the enemies of God—beginning with the Roman state—and establish God's kingdom. While Jesus readily identifies Himself as the Messiah (the Christ), He surprises everyone with the kind of Messiah He is. Instead of coming and demanding obedience as the Almighty Lord, He assumes the role of Servant as predicted in Isaiah (Isaiah 42:1-4; 49:1-6; 50:4-9; 53:1-12).

Wanting to take God on their own terms, many of Jesus' contemporaries, especially the religious establishment, misunderstood and rejected such a servant role for the Messiah. It is this very issue of Jesus' servanthood that continues to baffle people today, even people in the Church. While most of the world's religions present God as Sovereign Lord, only Christianity takes seriously His servanthood. As such, we follow Jesus' own proclamation that He "did not come to be served, but to serve" (Mark 10:45).

The question I would like to raise within *Knowing Jesus* is do we take Jesus' Lordship seriously enough to also take seriously His servanthood? Like most people, Peter resisted Jesus' service to him as evidenced by his initial refusal to let Jesus wash his feet (John 13:8). But Jesus is not a Lord, like other so-called lords, who require people to work dutifully on their behalf. As a matter of fact the true God will *not* be put into the position of an employer who needs others to make his business run. Instead God—and this is the essence of the Gospel message—turns the tables and works on *our* behalf (Isaiah 64:4).

Jesus as our servant does not mean that He is some kind of cosmic bellhop. Nor does it have anything to do with what is often called the "health and wealth gospel" which is no Gospel at all. *Jesus is the Lord who would be our servant.* His Lordship is the central fact of the universe. The real question we are left is: will we humbly trust Him to also be our servant? And while His service to us begins with His death on the cross, it continues to take place every moment of every day.

This profound insight, and the spiritual power which accompanies it, make for a most intriguing message from four unlikely authors. The following studies give each of those Gospel writers a brief opportunity to take the witness stand. As we elicit their testimony, we will discover just what it is about our Lord's servanthood that makes His message so compelling.

The Message of John
Receiving from Jesus

I f any of the Gospels provides a good starting place, John does: "In the beginning was the Word," he writes, offering a rather obvious parallel to the opening words from Genesis. In the first Genesis God spoke *creation* into existence, and in the "second Genesis" God speaks *redemption* into existence: "The Word became flesh and made His dwelling among us" (John 1:14).

That Word is not some superhuman being or archangel but none other than God Himself in His Son Jesus. And Jesus would bring God's re-creation power to a world racked by disease and despair, sin and sorrow. In their place He offered the Word of forgiveness and joy, healing and hope — namely, Himself.

It is with this One — Lamb, Living Water, Bread of Life, Light of the World, Gate, Good Shepherd, Resurrection and Life, Lord and Teacher, Way, Truth and Life, Vine — this God-Human that John would have his readers encounter. These things "are written," he states, "that you may believe that Jesus is the Christ, the Son of God, and that by believing you may have life in his name" (John 20:31).

Similar to other writers of the Gospels, John does not directly identify himself as author. He does, however, mention his own eyewitness familiarity with the events he describes (John 1:14; 19:35; 21:24), referring to himself as "the disciple whom Jesus loved" (John 20:2; 21:7, 20). Since the other three Gospels existed by the time John wrote — most likely around 90 A.D. — he felt little need to add another similar Gospel story.

Instead, John highlights Jesus' supernatural power and nature. In the first twelve chapters John describes seven miracles meant to authenticate the central fact of the Christian faith: Jesus is God. In chapters 13–17 he records Jesus' farewell discourse during the last supper, an event largely left out by Matthew, Mark, and Luke. Throughout his Gospel, John portrays Jesus as the provider for those who would receive His provision.

1
Having Our Thirst Quenched

John 4:1-26

Tony Campolo relates a conversation between himself and a young girl at an amusement park. As she held a huge cotton candy in her hand, he inquired how she could eat something that was almost as large as she. She replied that he just didn't understand: "I'm a lot bigger on the inside," she explained, "than I am on the outside."

And who can argue with this little girl's perspective? Whatever size we are on the outside, each of us is like a spiritual Grand Canyon on the inside. To expand Saint Augustine's famous insight a bit, that internal void which yearns to be filled may be *heart-shaped* but its also *canyon-sized*.

To read my Bible more, to pray more, to go to church more will not begin to fill this void. God is bigger and life is more complicated than such simplistic answers can satisfy. As a matter of fact, because Bible reading, prayer, and involvement with the Christian community gets us in touch with heaven, they increase (rather than fulfill) our thirst for the reality of communion with God. Only heaven will do that.

Those of us who are the most satisfied with life—and I include myself—are often the most shallow of people. We simply have little grasp of how utterly short this world's existence comes when compared to the goodness God will give us in His presence for eternity—an eternity He is preparing for us to share with Him.

Now do I need to take the book of Ecclesiastes off my reading list, or is it true that life includes *lots* of disappointment and pain? Surely God wants us to rise above everyday griefs. But it is in recognizing that our endeavors and relationships are filled with frustration and difficulty that we can begin to see some honest options.

If you are in touch with the void in your soul, if you are confused, disappointed, and pain-ridden, take heart. You have recognized the truth of Scott Peck's now famous understatement: "Life is difficult." But how, once we've found that door to reality, do we avoid total despair and instead open the door to something better?

The encounter between Jesus and a Samaritan woman in John 4 provides a place to start. Steeped in hurt and despair, this woman had built an almost impenetrable defense of self-protection. Any strategy which helped avoid bumping up against the ache inside was preferable to staring into the black hole of her soul. But she had one thing going for her: a willingness to stay and hear Jesus out. She would not leave disappointed.

1. What is something that disappoints you about life?

Read aloud John 4:1-26

2. The residents of Samaria were considered half-bred Jews because of interracial marriages with Gentiles. Many Jews would even travel around Samaria to avoid contact. What kind of prejudices does Jesus break down by entering into conversation with this woman?

3. Notice verses 6-7. The woman comes to the well alone at the sixth hour (noon). Why do you think she came alone to draw water at the hottest time of the day?

4. Instead of telling her right away who He was, Jesus began by asking the woman a favor (verses 7-9). What does this reveal about Jesus' understanding of meeting people's needs?

5. Look more carefully at verses 10-15. Describe the course of the conversation as it increasingly moves into deeper levels.

Why do you think the woman misses Christ's meaning about living water?

6. When did you first hear about Jesus, and what were your impressions of Him?

7. During their conversation about living water, Jesus delves into the woman's personal life (verses 16-18). Why?

8. What are specific areas of life in which people you know are "thirsty"?

9. Although Jesus speaks frankly about the woman's lifestyle, she does not respond defensively. What is it about Jesus that helps her open up to Him?

10. Study verses 19-24. The Samaritans worshiped on Mount Geri-
    zim; the Jews in Jerusalem. How does Jesus deal with the wom-
    an as she tried to side-step the main topic of their conversation?

11. Read verses 25-26 again. Why do you think Jesus waits until the
    end of the conversation to reveal who He is?

12. What is one way Jesus has brought satisfaction into your life?

    In what way do you feel thirsty right now for what Jesus
    offers?

For Further Reflection

Only occasionally, and then during personal crisis, are we overwhelmed by our own needs. Spend some time journaling (and sharing with others) using these questions:

✦ What are my deepest disappointments and hurts in life?

✦ What would it mean to open myself to Jesus' healing touch?

2
Getting Our Hunger Satisfied

John 4:27-42

I'm a nervous wreck," she told me. "For the last few months our family has been involved in an 'adopt-a-prisoner' ministry." She went on to explain, "The program includes regularly bringing 'your prisoner' home. Now we've just realized the woman is stealing from us and every time I leave home, I wonder what will be missing next!"

In my mind I was thinking, "Yeah, Juanita, that's what happens when you get involved in helping people like that. You ought to bail out."

My confident analysis did not last long, however. As she took a breath, Juanita's next statement took me completely off guard: "But you know, Bill, I wouldn't trade this experience for the world. Our entire family has never been more committed together and in prayer than we are right now."

People who take risks in applying the second great commandment often get taken—whether its *taken for granted* or *taken advantage* of. But they also avoid something worse: the risk of not loving others. Have you ever heard an older person express regret over the way he has lived his life? Few such confessions include, "I wish I had avoided loving people so much." We are not talking about "door-mat theology" here but genuine faith, hope, and love.

The further discomforting truth, though, is how closely tied the second commandment—loving others—is to the first commandment—loving God. Jesus goes so far as to say that feeding the hungry, housing the stranger, clothing the needy, looking after the sick, and visiting the prisoner constitute acts of love toward Him: "Whatever you did for one of the least of these brothers of mine, you did for Me" (Matthew 25:40). And even more sobering, neglecting such acts is equivalent to neglecting Him (Matthew 25:45).

But Jesus also promised that "It is more blessed to give than to receive" (Acts 20:35). When born out of trust in God, loving others does not leave us with a deficit. We very well may get taken advantage of as Juanita experienced. But we also get something more: the blessing and power of God.

1. What is something in life that energizes and motivates you?

Read aloud John 4:27-42

2. Why were the disciples surprised to find Jesus with this woman?

Why do you think they kept their thoughts to themselves?

3. Leaving her water jar behind, the woman goes back to tell people in her town about the remarkable man she has met at the well. Describe the conversation about food between Jesus and His disciples. (See verses 31-34.)

4. Review John 4:10-15. In what ways was the woman confused about the nature of living water?

How, apparently, were the disciples confused about "living food?" (4:31-34)

5. Given Jesus' encounter with the woman, what was it that gave Him the same kind of satisfaction that food gives a hungry person?

6. How does Jesus' way of meeting the needs of people challenge you?

7. Jesus continues to expand the metaphor of food by referring to its production in verses 35-38. In what way does He convey a sense of urgency and blessing to the task of making the needs of the people a priority for the disciples?

8. Note verses 39-42. What were the results of the woman's testimony to her village?

9. Notice the woman's state as we met her in John 4:7 and what is happening in her life by verse 42. What is the significance of meeting Jesus for this woman?

10. How can you identify with the woman in the ways you have experienced Christ's grace in your life?

11. In what ways would you like to take on a renewed urgency for God's work in the lives of people around you?

For Further Reflection

We all have unique "love frames." What happens inside that frame speaks love to us. Other actions, no matter how pleasant, do not carry the same impact.

✦ Write down the key people in your life, beginning with your family.

✦ Find a time when you can ask each one, "What are things I could do for you that would communicate my love, appreciation, and respect for you?" (If appropriate, tell that person what actions help you to feel loved.)

3
Letting Jesus Wash Our Feet

John 13:1-17

I like the poster that says, "There are two governing principles in the universe: Number One: There is a God. Number Two: You are not He." Trying to one-up God or even help Him out is like asking Bill Gates if he needs a loan. Only if you didn't know that Mr. Gates owns a huge chunk of Microsoft stock, worth billions of dollars, would you risk such an insult?

When it comes to finishing the Great Commission, for instance, God does not need us. He could, after all, finish the job with a few evangelistic stones! (Luke 3:8) To quote Paul's famous sermon on Mars Hill, "[God] is not served by human hands, as if He needed anything" (Acts 17:25). Our attempt to serve Him resembles the dilemma children face deciding what Christmas present to get for a father "who has everything." How do you serve someone who has absolutely no needs?

The simple answer is that we can't serve Him in the normal way service is understood. As a matter of fact, the God who is the Father of our Lord Jesus Christ is the servant—not the one served (Mark 10:45). And He will not relinquish that role to anyone.

"But we can and should serve God," someone will be quick to challenge. Didn't Paul describe himself in Galatians 1:10 as a servant of the Lord? Doesn't the Bible promote the idea that we are His servants, even for all eternity? (Revelation 22:3) The answer is, yes, Christians are God's servants, but *the way* we serve God cannot in

25

any way imply that He needs our service. True service to God begins with the sure knowledge that I am the receiver in God's economy, not the giver. I have the needs; He has the resources. Our service comes out of our need to experience God's help, not because He needs our help.

Have you been to a doctor recently? Why did you go? A while back I got a terrible pain in my chest. The pain grew so intense that at 3:00 in the morning I decided to go to the emergency room of the hospital. I didn't think it had anything to do with my heart. But I wanted to make sure and, fortunately, the pain was from a virus.

Why, though, did I go to the doctor? For his happiness and welfare, to make *him* well? No, for *my* welfare. And that's why we should go to Jesus, the Great Physician. I had nothing to offer my doctor but a willingness to listen and follow his prescription — to obey. We have nothing to offer Jesus but our willingness to follow His prescription for recovery.

But the fact that we are entirely unneeded (though not unwanted) and entirely beholden to God grates hard on our pride. Instead of acting as the humble recipients we are, we would prefer to die in service as heroes for God. "Ask not what God can do for you," we would chant, "but what you can do for God." Peter epitomizes our struggle with pride, and Jesus waits for the opportune moment to confront it.

1. In what ways does being the recipient of a gift, particularly an expensive one, make you uncomfortable?

Read aloud John 13:1-17

2. This event takes place during the last supper Jesus and His disciples have together. What actions here reveal Jesus as a servant?

3. Imagine yourself as one of the disciples watching Jesus prepare Himself to wash feet. How would you have reacted as He prepared?

4. How does Peter react when Jesus gets to him?

   Why would Peter be so uncomfortable about having Jesus wash his feet?

5. Jesus' reply in verse 8, that Peter must be a willing receiver, is straightforward. Why did Jesus tell Peter it was essential to let Him wash his feet?

   In what ways might this experience prepare Peter spiritually for the meaning of Jesus' death on the cross which would take place the very next day?

6. Like Peter, most people, given the choice, would rather take the servant role and wash Jesus' feet. Are you uncomfortable with the *idea* of being the one served by God rather than the one serving God? Explain.

   Describe some of your *feelings* about being a recipient rather than the giver in your relationship with God.

7. Focus on verses 9-10. If Jesus' role in washing people's feet

represents His servanthood in their lives, why would He not need to wash anything else?

8. Review verses 11-17. What is significant about Jesus washing Judas' feet and then saying His act provided them an example?

9. Luke records that the disciples had just been arguing over which one would be greatest in Jesus' coming kingdom (Luke 22:24). How does Jesus' actions here destroy any basis for pride?

10. Why is it critical that service for others comes out of an ongoing experience of being served by Jesus?

How could a greater awareness of being served by Jesus energize your service to others?

For Further Reflection

✦ *Do you want to give Jesus something?* He will gladly receive anything that shows your dependency and His sufficiency. Take some time to think of things to give Him. Hint: Give Him your anxieties—He'd take those. And how about your lack of ability and self-control, your fears, your weaknesses? It is with these He can prove His wisdom, control, courage, and strength. Remember, we serve God *not* by what we are willing to do for Him but by what we're willing to receive from Him.

✦ Use the following passages for reminders of the Lord's service to you: Isaiah 64:4, Jeremiah 29:11, and Romans 8:28.

The Message of Luke
Being Challenged by Jesus

Luke, an educated Greek physician and traveling companion to Paul, is the author of the book of Acts and also the Gospel that bears his name. (See Colossians 4:14 and Philemon 24.) Beside having a close relationship with Paul, Luke was acquainted with most of the key eyewitnesses who knew Jesus (Luke 1:1-4). After extensive interviews from these contacts Luke begins, "Since I myself have carefully investigated everything from the beginning, it seemed good also to me to write an orderly account" (Luke 1:3).

His account, most likely written between 65–80 A.D., proceeds as the most traditionally historical and biographical of the four Gospels. He, for instance, is the only writer to mention a Roman emperor's name. Of his many references to contemporary events and rulers which can be checked out, all have registered 100 percent accurate.

Using his considerable literary skills, Luke highlights Jesus' ministry as One who "came to seek and to save what was lost" (Luke 19:10). Maybe as the only Gentile in an all-Jewish cast of New Testament writers, Luke felt even more appreciation for the inclusiveness of Jesus' message. He places special emphasis on how Jesus brought salvation to the underprivileged and outsiders: children, women, flagrant sinners, Samaritans, and Gentiles.

People found by Jesus begin a new life filled with new priorities. Luke himself had his life's endeavors forever altered as he joined Paul starting with his second missionary trip (Acts 16:10; 20:5; 27:2). Near the end of his life Paul found Luke's high level of commitment of great comfort: "Only Luke is with me" (2 Timothy 4:11).

Now Luke would have the world wrestle with Jesus' challenge. He begins with his friend Theophilus to whom the Gospel and Acts are both addressed (Luke 1:3; Acts 1:1). Whether we are more like the unforgiving older brother or the wayward prodigal son, Jesus' call to respond interrupts despair with joy: "We had to celebrate and be glad, because this brother of yours was dead and is alive again; he was lost and is found" (Luke 15:32).

4
Receiving a Change of Vocation

Luke 5:1-11

It became real for me when I saw the auction notice in the newspaper. All my friend's dairy farm implements were to be sold. Twenty years of hard work by the seven family members could not overcome an ill-timed expansion through debt and a few years of chronically low milk prices.

They were the most solid of community and church members with a well-managed operation and a herd numbering close to two hundred. Dairy farming was in the blood of this Dutch family. Great-grandfather, grandfather, father, brothers—all found success in it. The last thing I thought possible was bankruptcy.

But the farm was sold: the creditors were paid while the fifty-year-old husband and father of the family busied himself looking for work and a place to relocate. As the day of sale and departure grew near, I could sense the stress, blanketed with the sorrow of regret. Yet there was something else in the air as well. Relief and acceptance of their fate, yes. But there was something even more positive.

The best way I can describe it is a sense of *rare opportunity*. Rare, because no one before now could envision the family doing anything but dairy farming. They were Dutch dairy farmers, pure and simple. But now there were no more cows to milk, and life was far from pure and simple. With no script to follow the family was wide open for new experiences, and they sensed it more than anyone. This was going to be scary, but it would not be boring.

Scripture is full of people who made radical vocational changes. Noah turned to boat building at midlife. Moses started out as prince, turned shepherd, turned deliverer, turned administrator. Jesus himself left the familiarity of carpentry for other, more profitable pursuits.

One of the most intriguing vocational changes Scripture records is that of Peter. His rather radical job change brought with it a similar mixture of fear and excitement. But it brought something more as well: *rare opportunity*.

1. If you could have any job in the world, what choice would you make?

Read aloud Luke 5:1-11

2. Describe what is happening in the opening scene.

3. What requests does Jesus make of Peter in verses 3 and 4?

4. If you were Peter, how would you have have responded to Jesus' request in verse 4?

Why do you imagine Peter went along with this?

5. Describe the catch of fish and Peter's response to it.

Why do you think this miracle caused such a strong reaction on Peter's part?

6. Peter used a different title for Jesus in verse 8 than he had in verse 5. What is significant about the change?

7. In Luke 4:38-39, Peter had witnessed the healing of his mother-in-law. Why do you think that he apparently did not respond to Jesus then — but does so now?

What is an area of your life that if God worked miraculously it would get your attention in a hurry?

8. Note Peter's fear in verse 8. Why can coming to grips with the concept that Jesus is Lord be frightening?

9. As we consider following Jesus fully in a particular area of life, He offers Peter (and us) a word of assurance: "Don't be afraid. . . ." How can this assurance help you move ahead in your relationship with Jesus?

10. Again note the two requests Jesus made of Peter in verses 3 and 4. How would you describe Jesus' final challenge for Peter in verse 10?

   What is significant about this challenge coming at this point in the story?

11. Jesus offers Peter a new vocation: catching people for God's kingdom. What intrigues or encourages you to make a deeper commitment to Jesus in His fishing enterprise?

For Further Reflection

✦ If Peter's fishing business was a central area of his life, what is a similarly important area for you? (for example, your job, your studies, family, future goals, relationship with another person)?

✦ Where is Jesus in relation to your "fishing business"? Explain.

___ Nowhere in sight
___ On the horizon
___ Approaching the boat
___ One foot in, one foot out
___ Fully in

✦ What would it mean for you to invite Jesus to be fully involved in your "fishing business"?

5
Sitting at Jesus' Feet

Luke 10:25-42

Beware of anything that competes with loyalty to Jesus Christ."
This statement introduces a challenging declaration by Oswald Chambers. But how do you imagine he will finish it?
What competitors to Jesus will he encourage us to avoid? Will he remind us to stay away from time-wasting leisure activities or immersion into our jobs or old habits that pull us down?

No, he is about to warn us of a much more subtle and insidious rival: *"The greatest competitor to devotion to Jesus is service for Him."*

If you're like me, it may take a moment for this thought to sink in but as it does, its truth becomes inescapable. So often we find ourselves caught up in *doing* the Christian life that we find little time left for simply *being with* the One who called us into this life.

In his helpful book, *Ordering Your Private World,* Gordon MacDonald identifies a "doing" versus "being" lifestyle with the term *drivenness. Driven people* live stressful lives which can erupt into fits of anger and intolerance. They define who they are by what they do and thus have a constant need to succeed. Highly competitive, they look for satisfaction through winning approval of others; they often use people in their drive to the top.

A lifestyle of *calledness,* in contrast, cultivates inner peace that gives balance and pace to life. *Called people* are confident and content with whom God has made them to be and thus resist the need for

self-promotion. Faithfulness and stewardship are values they up-
hold. Called people are teachable and accountable to others.

Being called and being driven are on two opposite sides of a contin-
uum. Each of us finds ourselves fluctuating somewhere in between.
In our "fast-forwarded lives," it seems almost impossible to cut
through the clamor of other voices vying for our attention to hear
that "still, small voice."

Martha's and Mary's encounter with Jesus in Luke 10:38-42 raises
questions that can help us identify our own struggle with drivenness
and embrace a sense of calling.

1. What are the things that bring the most time pressure into your
   life?

Read aloud Luke 10:38-42

2. Describe the relationship between the people in this story.

3. Martha, as the older sister, is responsible for extending hospitality to at least thirteen guests—Jesus and His disciples. What
   appears to be on Martha's mind as she makes preparations?

4. Put yourself in Martha's place. What tensions do you find yourself in when you act as host or hostess of a large gathering and
   meal?

5. How would you describe Martha's reaction to Mary?

What kind of feelings do you sense in her plea to Jesus?

6. What kind of pressure situations tempt you to tell the Lord what He should do rather than listen to Him?

7. Paraphrase in your own words Jesus' response to Martha in verses 41-42.

8. Jesus said in verse 42, "Mary has chosen what is better." How is Mary a model of Jesus' priorities for these sisters?

9. What does the act of sitting at someone's feet suggest?

What kind of things does "sitting at Jesus' feet" mean for us?

10. Skim the parable of the Good Samaritan in the previous passage (verses 25-37). If Martha, in extending hospitality, is an example of Jesus' teaching about being a Good Samaritan, why do you think He rebukes her now?

11. How do you find yourself caught up in the "Martha syndrome"—serving Jesus while neglecting to sit at His feet?

12. How should "serving" and "sitting" relate to each other in the Christian life?

13. How can you develop a more "sitting lifestyle" given the particular pressures of your world?

For Further Reflection

✦ Test your drivenness: On a scale of 1 to 10 (1 as definitely no, 10 as definitely yes), how would you rate your own sense of drivenness in each of the following areas:

___ Is time for cultivating your relationship with God often crowded out by the demands of a busy schedule?

___ Are you consistently preoccupied with anxiety?

___ Do you easily become critical?

___ Do you tell the Lord what to do rather than listen to what He has to say?

___ Are you serving God more and enjoying it less?

___ SUBTOTAL ÷ 5 = ___ TOTAL RATE OF DRIVENNESS

✦ How do you feel about your present rate of drivenness?

✦ What are some specific things you can do to develop a deeper sense of "calledness" in your life?

✦ A last thought on being called:
"One of the desert fathers expressed it simply but powerfully. Into a jar he poured water and some sand. As he shook the jar, the water became murky, but as he allowed the jar to rest, the sand settled to the bottom and the water became clear again. Using this visual aid, he taught his disciples that the pace people live their lives normally clouds their spiritual perspective. Those who dare to settle themselves into God's stillness find that the water of perception becomes clear again."
  —Joyce Huggett, *Listening to God*

6
Spending Like There's No Tomorrow

Luke 19:11-27

I grew up watching "I Love Lucy." Actually I watched "The Lucy Show" which aired from 1962–68 and reruns of "I Love Lucy" which originally aired a decade earlier. As a kid in the '60s I was really into the space program, and I have a particularly fond memory of a Lucy show where she thought she was being asked by the government to become an astronaut. Maybe you remember, too.

As Lucy anxiously prepared to do patriotic service for her country, she courageously stood at attention and quoted president John F. Kennedy: "Ask not what your country can do for you; ask what you can do for your country." But true to most Lucy plots, her preparations for the space trip started to unravel and her frustration rose. Finally in great exasperation, she looked right at the television audience and asked, "What more could that man in the White House want from me?"

I don't know if I loved Lucy, but I enjoyed Lucy because she made me laugh. After her death I was surprised to come upon this statement: "I am not funny," she told an interviewer in 1983. "My writers were funny. My directors were funny. The situations were funny. . . ."

But there must be something more that contributed to her incredible popularity—the kind of popularity that literally stopped the nation during the '50s every Monday night from 9–9:30. "What I am," she went on to say, "is brave. I have never been scared. Not when I did movies, certainly not when I was a model, and not when I did 'I Love Lucy.' "

If you believe Lucy, and I think I do, her success came less because of her abilities and more because of her courage. She had guts. This quality is the most common of all qualities shared by people who accomplish something.

Scripture is full of people who had guts. Maybe we would call it spiritual guts. One of these risk-takers is an unlikely man named Zacchaeus. Zacchaeus acquired his considerable wealth from his job as chief tax collector for the Roman government. It is an understatement to say his occupation did not earn him a lot of love or respect from his fellow Jews. Most likely they labeled him a cheat and a traitor.

But Jesus wanted to have lunch with him. After what must have been an extraordinary encounter, Zacchaeus decided to remove himself from the rolls of the rich: "Look, Lord!" he said in Luke 19:8, "Here and now I give half of my possessions to the poor, and if I have cheated anybody out of anything, I will pay back four times the amount." Can you see the *Jerusalem News* headlines: "Luncheon with Jesus Changes Zacchaeus from Fat Cat to Thin Kittie!"

No one in the crowd that day expected such a radical response from Zacchaeus. People could understand the rich young ruler's sorrowful departure from Jesus which Luke records just prior to the Zacchaeus story. But Zacchaeus' response seems so out of character, that the people who heard his words were undoubtedly surprised by his decision.

To correct the crowd's understanding of the radical nature of God's kingdom, Jesus tells *The Parable of the Minas*. This parable explains why people like Zacchaeus would make such a response to Jesus. Let's have a look ourselves.

1. What is the most risk-taking act you have done in the last few years?

Read aloud Luke 19:11-27

2. Describe the events of the story involving the nobleman and his servants.

3. The mina, according to the NIV footnotes, was worth about three months' wages. What kind of investment do you imagine the first two servants made with their mina during the king's absence?

   How does the king respond to their efforts?

4. In *The Parable of the Talents* (Matthew 25:14-30), each servant is given a different number of talents: five, two, and one. The different amounts given represent *varying abilities*. In *The Parable of the Minas*, however, each servant is given the same number of minas: one — which can be interpreted as *our life*. If the mina represents a person's life, what point is made here about the need to invest it?

5. The first servant received a 1000 percent and the second a 500 percent return on their investments. Such an incredible return indicates that they were willing to take a large risk with the king's money. What do you think gave them the security to take such a risk?

6. On a scale of one to ten (one being least and ten most) how much of a risk-taker are you? Explain.

7. In contrast to the first two servants, what kind of attitude toward life does the third servant represent?

8. Reread verses 20-21 where the third servant explains his actions to the king. If the king represents the Lord, what kind of view of God does he have?

How does his view of God explain his actions?

9. How does our view of God influence our life?

10. Focus on verses 20-26. Describe the king's reaction to the third servant.

    Why do you think the king takes away his mina and gives it to the one who has ten?

11. Illustrate what you have seen happen both negatively and positively to people who take risks in investing their lives?

12. What is a spiritually productive risk or investment of yourself you would like to make this next month? (Particularly consider an investment you could make in the life of another person.)

For Further Reflection

✦ Consider "The Rose," a song popularized by Bette Midler.

It's the heart afraid of breaking that never learns to dance.
It's the dream afraid of waking that never takes the chance.
It's the one who won't be taken who cannot seem to give.
And the soul afraid of dying that never learns to live.[1]

What, according to this song, are the consequences of *not* taking risks?

✦ Brainstorm on one or two spiritually oriented risks which would cause you to place more dependence on the Lord.

---

1. *THE ROSE*, by Amanda McBroom. Copyright © 1977 Warner-Tamerlane Publishing Corp. (BMI) and Third Story Music Inc. (BMI), c/o Warner-Tamerlane Publishing Corp. All Rights Reserved. Used by Permission of WARNER BROS. PUBLICATIONS INC., Miami, FL 33014

The Message of Matthew
Learning from Jesus

Though the Gospel of Mark was most likely written first, the early church placed Matthew first in the New Testament canon. Whereas Mark explains Jewish customs, Matthew assumes his readers already understand them. (See Matthew 15:2 and 23:27.) Matthew shows particular interest in identifying how Jesus fulfilled Old Testament prophecy. From these observations, most have concluded that the Gospel was initially written for Jewish Christians. So it makes sense to place it as the first Gospel because it highlights the interconnectedness of the Old and New Testaments.

The date and authorship of Matthew are the most difficult to pin down of all the Gospels. Arguments can be made to place it as early as 65 A.D. and as late as 110. Matthew's name was affixed to the Gospel in the early second century. Since he was not a prominent disciple, this fact alone supports his having a key role in its origin. If Matthew did not actually write it, very likely he led the community out of which it emerged or played an important part in its collection and distribution.

Out of his life as a tax collector (Matthew 9:9-13), Jesus called Matthew to be a member of the Twelve. We can imagine the initial friction between Matthew, a man considered a traitor for the Roman government, and Peter, a loyal Jew. But forgiveness and reconciliation lay at the heart of Jesus' message, and before it could be communicated to those outside, it must start among the Twelve.

For young Christians, Matthew's systematic arrangement of Jesus' teaching provided a great tutorial of the Christian life. *The Sermon on the Mount* (chapters 5–7) quite possibly constitutes the greatest expression of love for God and love for people ever penned.

Matthew invites his readers to enroll in the school of life. In this school the Teacher is also the Subject who makes an offer hard to refuse: "Come to me, all you who are weary and burdened, and I will give you rest. Take my yoke upon you and learn from me, for I am gentle and humble at heart, and you will find rest for your souls. For my yoke is easy and my burden is light" (Matthew 11:28-30).

7
Pursuing the Things Worthy of Pursuit

Matthew 16:13-28

I knew I should not have done it but, of course, hindsight is 20/20. My girlfriend Teresa, soon to be my fiancée, soon to be my wife, was already demonstrating Job-like patience; waiting ever so sensitively for me to get around to asking her to marry me.

So the announcement came—at least that's what she thought. As I handed her a small wrapped box, I said that it had something to do with carrots. Little did I anticipate the racing of a young woman's mind between being handed such a gift and the unwrapping of it.

When the box revealed an enormous, gum-ball machine ring, the disappointed response just didn't correspond to my humorous intentions when I wrapped it. I guess I found out she really liked me, though. When it was all said and done, she still wanted to marry me and was willing to wait yet again for a young man to gather the courage to ask for what he wanted.

Important announcements should be treated carefully. They can be significant moments not just because they convey a previously made decision to the audience, but because they solidify a commitment for the announcer. When a decision is announced publicly, it becomes encased as the person's firmly held commitment or belief. Sure there can be reversal or change of mind, but such backtracking will come at a high social price.

Jesus knew relatively early in His ministry that many were beginning to announce their belief or lack of belief about whether He was the long-promised Messiah. Their pronouncements showed a wide degree of impressions that He had left on people. There were twelve men, however, who He really wanted to get it right.

So He waited for the right time to ask them, "But what about you? Who do you say that I am?" Their declaration did not settle all the issues or keep the disciples from vacillating—as subsequent events clearly reveal. But the announcement becomes a turning point for them and their leader, Peter. Now Jesus would be able to build on a commitment, spoken however tentatively, but all the same spoken aloud for all within earshot to hear.

1. When have you said something aloud that helped you carry through on a decision that had been personal up to that point?

Read aloud Matthew 16:13-28

2. John the Baptist had been executed by King Herod, and the Jewish religious leaders were growing increasingly hostile to Jesus. What do you think it meant for the disciples to hear Peter verbalize their answer to Jesus' question in verse 15?

3. In verses 17-19, Jesus responds to Peter's declaration with an announcement of His own. What do you think Jesus' words would have meant to His disciples?

4. Review verses 20-21. Why do you think Jesus now felt free to clearly identify His mission?

In what ways did Jesus' mission not fit Jewish expectations of the coming Messiah?

5. Describe in your own words Jesus' reaction when Peter seeks to correct Him.

How can Jesus' characterization of Peter in verse 23 make sense in light of what He said about Peter in verses 17-19?

6. What about Jesus and His ministry do you find most difficult or disturbing?

7. Reread verses 24-28. How would you describe Christ's teaching on discipleship as it is presented here?

8. Jesus' description of the costs and benefits to following Him begins with denying yourself. How could self-denial ultimately result in self-benefit?

9. What does it mean to "take up your cross"?

How could the paradox of losing your life actually make it possible to save and find it?

10. How have you seen the benefits of following Jesus come through in your own life?

What is a struggle in your life in which you need reassurance that the benefits of following Jesus outweigh the costs involved?

For Further Reflection

✦ Make a public announcement. First, write down a *realistic commitment* you would like to make but are finding difficult to follow. Begin with the words: "With God's help I will. . . ."

✦ Then present this to a friend or the group and ask them to keep you accountable until completed.

8
Coming Down off the Mountaintop

Matthew 17:1-20

What are some of your New Year's resolutions of years gone by? What is your record of the one most quickly broken after midnight, December thirty-first?

Everyone is wary of New Year's resolutions. We see so little evidence that such commitments have much staying power. And who of us cannot remember making a commitment at an inspiring conference or weekend retreat only to find a letdown in willpower when we rejoined our normal life?

This is not to say that we should avoid these emotional and spiritual experiences. Often they act as turning points in our understanding of how to live out what we know to be true. Our failure to follow through simply points out the truth of Jesus' statement that "the spirit is willing, but the body is weak."

If there is any danger in spiritually uplifting experiences, maybe it is in the subtle attitude of presumption that creeps in. Spiritual power is not born from confidence in a newfound emotional energy but from a faith that is poor in spirit and therefore looks to God for sustenance. To put it in biblical terms, "God opposes the proud but gives grace to the humble" (James 4:6; Proverbs 3:34). In our study from Matthew 17 we will see Jesus' disciples experience both the mountaintop of excitement and the valley of despair. It should prove helpful as we seek to humbly pursue God's grace through the highs and lows of our own experiences.

1. What were some of the spiritual high points in your life?

What happened when the intensity of the high wore off?

Read aloud Matthew 17:1-13

2. In the previous passage, Peter has just verbalized his belief in Jesus as the Messiah. Now Jesus takes Peter, James, and John on a trip they will never forget. How is the experience described?

3. How does Peter react to what happens?

What do you imagine would have gone through your mind if you had been there?

4. Moses represents the Old Testament Law and Elijah represents the Prophets. What does Jesus' appearance with them signify?

How is Jesus unique among the three?

5. Look again at Matthew 16:28. How might Jesus' transfiguration fulfill this intriguing statement?

6. According to Malachi 4:5-6, the prophet Elijah would return to inaugurate a kingdom headed up by the Messiah. In what ways did John the Baptist's ministry fulfill the prophecy concerning Elijah's coming?

   How did John's ministry and the treatment he received prefigure Jesus?

7. The voice from heaven in verse 5 says, "This is my Son, whom I love; with Him I am well pleased. Listen to Him!" What must this have meant to Jesus?

   What are its implications for those of us who claim to be His disciples?

Read aloud Matthew 17:14-20

8. Jesus descends the mountain and finds the crowd, a father, his demon-possessed son, and nine disciples. What kind of attitude must Jesus have sensed to prompt the rebuke He gave in verse 17?

Why might a presumptuous attitude interfere with the disciples' ability to heal the boy?

9. How would you describe mustard-seed faith?

Why is it so powerful?

10. In what situations are you tempted to exercise a "presumptuous faith" that takes God for granted?

What happens to your faith when circumstances turn against you?

11. What is an issue in your life in which God is calling you to exercise "dependent faith"?

For Further Reflection

Take some time to journal with the following in mind: Describe the difference between having a *good* day and having a *dependent* day — a day when you exercise trust in the Lord.

9

Counting the Costs and the Benefits

Matthew 19:13-30

Often I give my wife Teresa flowers on our wedding anniversary. Often, but not every year. Why? Because it so easily becomes an expected event—not so much from her point of view but from mine: "Honey, over the last umpteen years I've given you flowers on our wedding anniversary. And because you're my wife and it is that time of the year, I thought it my duty to give you flowers once again. Here, I hope you enjoy them." How do you think she would respond to such a "gift"?

From what I've seen, much of our obedience to God resembles such flower giving. We, in effect, say, "God, because you deserve my attention, my prayers, my good attitudes . . . here they are." But is God any more pleased by flowers given to Him out of obligation or obedience from a sense of duty than a wife or girlfriend would be?

Webster defines duty as "any action required by one's position or by moral or legal considerations." Herein is the rub: "required." Doing something because it is your duty is very different from doing something because it is your desire. A country may *hire* soldiers as mercenaries—those paid to fight. We will *respect* these soldiers who do their duty by risking their lives in line of combat. But we will *admire* soldiers who volunteer for a dangerous mission. We even give them medals when they take a substantial risk to life and limb because we recognize a degree of bravery that is beyond duty.

What lies beyond being *a mercenary* (doing what you're paid to do) and beyond duty (doing what you're expected to do) is *desire* (doing what you want to do.)

Motivation from duty or desire has to do with perspective. If I do something because it is required or expected, I either feel guilty for saying "no," or I resent the entrapment I feel for saying "yes." So often we do something because of the requirement itself and not because of the benefit that requirement brings. When our actions are detached from fulfillment, they become empty obligation.

Spiritual obligation is the drudgery that comes in duty without devotion, ritual without relationship, effort without affection. In Psalm 51:16-17, David spoke for God when he declared: "You do not delight in sacrifice, or I would bring it; you do not take pleasure in burnt offerings. The sacrifices of God are a broken spirit; a broken and contrite heart, O God, you will not despise."

Desire develops as we remind ourselves of the benefit we receive. Jesus' message, more often than not, was just this: *Count the benefits.* Sure there are costs to following Him, but it is infinitely more costly not to. Failing to follow Jesus, not the reverse, is the only real cause for talking about sacrifice.

Operating from a "benefits mentality" rather than from a "cost mentality" has far-reaching implications for how we seek to motivate ourselves and others. Jesus is more than happy to show us the way.

1. What is something you own which would be difficult to give away? Explain.

Read aloud Matthew 19:13-30

2. How was the disciples' view of children in conflict with Jesus' view?

3. After the incident with the children, a man came to Jesus. What did he have going for him?

4. Study verse 21. Describe Jesus' challenge to this young man.

   Why do you think Jesus required the man to make such a clear-cut choice?

5. The commandments that Jesus cites in verse 18 have to do with our relationships with people. How does Jesus' challenge to the man relate to the commandments that the man does not cite? (See Exodus 20:1-12 if you need.)

6. What do you see in the way Jesus relates to this man that could inform us about how to communicate the Gospel message?

   When do you think such a direct style is appropriate and when is it not appropriate?

7. Jesus offered the man a superior kind of treasure. In light of this, why do you think that the man found it impossible to take up the challenge to sell, give, and follow?

8. In Jesus' day wealth was considered a sign of God's favor. How would you describe Jesus' view of wealth according to verses 21-26?

9. In what ways do you struggle with the issue of wealth and possessions?

10. Focus on verse 27. Do you think Peter's question to Jesus is appropriate? Explain.

The hundred-times return that Jesus mentions in verse 29 is actually 10,000 percent. In what ways have you experienced the truth of what Jesus describes?

11. Why would Jesus use such blatant self-interest to motivate first the rich man and now the disciples?

12. Do you find yourself following Jesus more out of dutiful obedience or a self-interested desire?

What helps to ignite the flames of desire for God in your life?

For Further Reflection

✦ On a scale of one to ten (one being pure duty and ten pure desire) where are you in living your life as a Christian?

✦ Reflect on ways to "inflame your desires" for God. Read Isaiah 64:4. Write down all the ways you can think of that God is acting on your behalf.

The Message of Mark
Being Involved with Jesus

Mark's first sentence, "The beginning of the Gospel about Jesus Christ, the Son of God," has no verb. And his last sentence ends with three women fleeing Jesus' empty tomb "because they were afraid." In between, the author wastes no time moving in rapid-fire procession from one event to the next.

Jesus, from Mark's perspective, is a man of action. When He comes on the scene, the demonic world scatters, the religious world bristles, the political world stumbles, and a whole lot of people are healed, instructed, and challenged. Jesus' message: "The time has come. The kingdom of God is near. Repent and believe the good news!" (Mark 1:15)

Actually, Mark's perspective is almost universally recognized as the firsthand recollections of Jesus' lead disciple, Peter. Though not one of the Twelve, Mark may have become a Christian through Peter (1 Peter 5:13). He was a cousin to Barnabas and a traveling companion to both Peter and Paul. And although he had a famous falling-out with Paul (Acts 15:36-41), the two later reconciled (Colossians 4:10; 2 Timothy 4:11; Philemon 24).

Scholars differ as to when Mark wrote his Gospel, with a date between 55–60 A.D. representing a likely possibility. Broad agreement suggests Mark's Gospel as the earliest written account of Jesus; it may have served as a basis for the Gospels of Matthew and Luke. Keeping Old Testament quotations and allusions to a minimum while explaining Jewish customs (Mark 7:3, 11, for example) indicates a likelihood that Mark's audience was Gentile.

Knowing that believers throughout the Roman world faced severe persecution from the state, Mark focuses on Jesus as the Suffering Servant. But for those who would follow, the suffering of the Cross leads to the glories of the kingdom. And such Good News is not meant to be contained. For people who want their lives to count, Jesus' invitation includes a promise: "Come, follow me, and I will make you fishers of men" (Mark 1:17).

10
Managing Our Time, Jesus' Style

Mark 1:21-45

Iknew I was out of control when I found myself carrying on a conversation on my cordless telephone and trying to repark our car at the same time.

Maybe things are different for you. If you have a moment to leisurely sit back and focus on this study, totally free of distraction and without the gnawing thought that your life is crowded by other priorities vying for your attention—feel free to skip it and go on to the next one. Oh, before you do, take a moment to thank the Lord for having the good sense to pace yourself.

If you're like almost everyone else, you're wondering how you can keep your week together and balance the demands of work, getting the kids taxied around, washing the clothes, fixing that leaky faucet, planning for a weekend vacation, getting that medical checkup you've been putting off, studying the Bible or just doing some reading. . . . If that's more where you're at, then hang on—this study is for you.

There was an age when time was money with the equation weighted on the value of money. No longer. With the tremendous pressures of our modern society, we have run out of time and since value depends on scarcity, time's worth has skyrocketed. Time is now considered priceless.

"This sense of acceleration is not just a vague and spotted impression," says Nancy Gibbs in a *Time* magazine article. "In 1967, testimony before a Senate subcommittee indicated that by 1985 people could be working just 22 hours a week, or 27 weeks a year, or they could retire at age 38. This would leave only the great challenge of finding a way to enjoy all that leisure."

Instead what really happened, according to a Harris survey, is "the amount of leisure time enjoyed by the average American has shrunk 37 percent since 1973. Over the same period, the average workweek, including commuting, has jumped from under forty one hours to nearly forty seven hours. In some professions, predictably law, finance, and medicine, the demands often stretch to eighty-plus hours a week. Vacations have shortened to the point where they are frequently no more than long weekends. And the Sabbath is for — what else — shopping."[1]

Jesus did not live in a fast-paced culture like ours, but He faced another, more significant time issue: three short years to complete the story of salvation. Thirty-six months of ministry meant that a lot of people would go unhealed, untaught, and undiscipled. But at the end of His life, Jesus could still declare: "It is finished." He had not accomplished all He could have, but He accomplished all He needed to. Discerning His priorities in the quiet confines of communion with His Father made that crucial difference. It will for us as well.

1. In what kinds of situations do you feel pressured to do what's urgent rather than what's important?

Read aloud Mark 1:21-45

2. In what ways did Jesus' teaching differ from that of the scribes?

---

1. Nancy Gibbs, "How America Has Run Out of Time," *Time*, 29 April 1989, 58.

3. The evil spirits address Jesus by name with the apparent intention of trying to exercise control over Him. What is significant about Jesus turning the tables by usurping control over these spirits?

4. Verses 29-31 tell the story of Jesus healing Simon's mother-in-law. How would you describe this healing?

5. After a full day of powerful encounters described in verses 32-34, Jesus goes off the next morning by Himself for prayer. Why do you think He felt the need for this time with His Father?

6. In what ways are you frustrated or satisfied with your own prayer life?

7. Notice verse 37 where Peter finds Jesus. What is behind Peter's statement that "Everyone is looking for you!"?

8. Why might it be difficult for Jesus to say "no" in such a situation?

What difference do you think His prayer time with the Father made in helping Him to respond to the urgent demands of those around Him?

9. In verse 38 Jesus declares His overriding purpose. Why do you think preaching took on a higher priority for Him than working miracles?

10. How does Jesus' example of resisting urgent demands and pursuing important priorities challenge you?

11. What are some urgent demands in your life that need to be evaluated in the clarifying light of God's priorities?

12. What is one thing that, if you began today and kept doing it, would make a significant, positive difference in your life?

What stops you from doing this and what can get you going on it?

For Further Reflection

✦ Read Ecclesiastes 3:1-14 three times a day for one week and reflect on a God-centered perspective on *time*.

✦ When this is completed write down what you've learned and how it will affect your schedule.

11
Giving Others Something to Eat

Mark 6:6b-13, 30-44

Anumber of years ago our family moved from Portland to Eugene, Oregon. Our twenty-six-foot U-Haul became so crammed that we ended up leaving a table with friends. The table needed to be refinished, but its unique style with pull-out end boards and groove legs made it appealing. I liked it, and made plans to eventually retrieve it.

Our friends, Chuck and Camille, needed a dining room table so on their own they decided to refinish the table. The result: a stunning beauty. The problem: they didn't ask us first. When they did ask us about the table, they asked if they could have it for its pre-finished value. Now I had a problem. On the one hand I thought I ought to be generous and recognize that it was their efforts that increased by tenfold a $20 table. But then, wasn't that table mine? Didn't I own it? So I took the easy way out—I told them I'd think about it. Well, what would you have done?

What I realized was that I was in a no-win situation. There was no way I could give them the table cheerfully. I felt compelled, I felt squeezed. Chuck and Camille had been close friends for years but that was my table. It was no one's fault—these things happen. But how could I freely give them the table without harboring that little corner of resentment, knowing it was really taken rather than given? What should I do: give them the table and then pray that God would help me deal with lingering resentment that I was sure to have?

Maybe, but I just couldn't. So after a couple more weeks of procrastination, I wrote one of the most difficult letters of my life. I said in effect that I wanted the table back and that I'd be up the next week to get it. After finishing the letter I forced myself by an act of will to seal the envelope, put a stamp on it and slip it into a mailbox where I couldn't retrieve it.

I felt then, as I still feel, that you can't give something away you don't possess. If I didn't really believe I owned that table, I couldn't give it away freely and, under the circumstances, I didn't feel like I owned it.

It seems to me that a person who is under compulsion makes choices that are not motivated by love but by fear. It is not an act of love to walk the second mile or to give someone your cloak à la the *Sermon on the Mount.* If you feel like you have to, it's an act of compulsion.

Well, my letter generated another letter from them. I hesitated as I opened it. I didn't know what to expect. What they proposed was to pay me $150 to buy the table. Now I knew that they recognized that I owned the table. So I was free to give it. But of course, this presented an additional challenge. Now that I was in a position to give cheerfully, would I? The answer in this case: "Nothing would please me more." My cheerfulness was eclipsed only by my relief! I was reconciled to my conscience — and to my friends.

Scripture gives us powerful incentives to be generous with our money, our energy, and our time. It is the latter two that Jesus' disciples struggle with in the following passage.

1. What generally happens when you get overwhelmed and stretched beyond your limit?

Read aloud Mark 6:6b-13

2. How would you describe Jesus' instructions to the disciples?

3. How would limiting their supplies develop the kind of faith they were calling others to?

Limited supplies would also require them to be dependent on the people they were seeking to reach. How might such dependence increase the effectiveness of their ministry?

Read aloud Mark 6:30-44

4. Upon their return the disciples, now called apostles, were likely looking forward to some "R & R" time with Jesus. Instead, what actually takes place?

5. How would you describe the disciples' attitude toward the crowd?

What is Jesus' attitude toward the crowd?

6. Notice verse 37. Why do you think Jesus would say, "You give them something to eat"?

7. What is an area in your own life that you've felt the Lord challenging you to go beyond your "normal limits"?

8. How would you characterize the disciples' response to Jesus?

   What would have been a better response?

9. Jesus' question in verse 38 challenges the disciples to evaluate their resources. How is their situation similar to what they faced when He sent them out two by two?

10. Verse 34 describes the crowd as shepherdless sheep. In what ways do verses 39-44 express Jesus' role as the Shepherd?

11. More than anyone, the disciples must have gasped in astonishment as two fish and five loaves fed 5,000 men and their families. Interestingly, twelve baskets are left — one for each of the disciples. Upon reflection, what do you think the disciples learned from this experience?

12. What is something related to helping other people that you have a hard time trusting God for?

What might it mean to take a step of faith in this area?

For Further Reflection

✦ Think of someone you want to stretch yourself with in terms of service. What is something specific that would be of great help to that person?

✦ Plan a time and a way to make it happen.

12
Having Something to Remember

Mark 14:1-26

People walk by the spot everyday without giving it a second thought. They go about their day completely oblivious to one of my favorite places on the planet. That place is a simple landscaped garden on Pine Street next door to my boyhood home in Wooster, Ohio.

Actually, as I write this I am over 2,000 miles away and separated by more than a decade from my last visit there. But strong memories strengthened by periodic visits over the years melt my often hurried life with the simple joys of discovery made by the little boy who lived there. Here I go again; I've mentally transported myself back to Wooster, and I'm enjoying every moment of it.

Of course not all our memories provide such pleasurable association. But good or bad, memories form a powerful reservoir of sensations which provide direction to our life.

Old Testament prophets constantly reminded the people of Israel that their God was the same One who delivered their ancestors from the tyranny of Egypt. The broken bread and poured-out wine likewise provides Jesus' followers with a powerful reminder of His sacrifice for sin: "Do this," He told His disciples, "in remembrance of Me."

This guide's first two studies from John 4 introduced us to Jesus' offer of "living water" and "living food" for people who open their lives to His provision. Studies 3–11 revealed more about how to secure that provision. Now, in this study, we will see how the One who promises living water and living food is the One who also provides it.

1. Describe one of the important, positive memories of your childhood.

Read aloud Mark 14:1-11

2. These events begin the last few days of Jesus' life. Describe the diverse group of people identified in this passage.

3. What kind of intentions and plans do the chief priests, teachers of the law, and Judas have?

How are the woman's actions a dramatic contrast to these other plans?

4. The flask of pure nard likely amounted to the family's entire savings, valued at a year's wages. A debate broke out on the wisdom of its use in this way. Do you identify more with the "careful givers" or the "cheerful givers"?

5. Jesus says that a legitimate concern for the poor would not, in this case, include giving them money from potential sale of the perfume. Why?

6. How, according to Jesus, are the woman's actions significant?

Read aloud Mark 14:12-26

7. What do you think the disciples were thinking as they gathered for this meal?

In verse 19, the response that a betrayer exists among them does not bring outrage but sadness and self-reflection. Why?

8. As thousands of Jewish households remember God's deliverance through the Exodus, Jesus attaches a very different meaning to the bread and cup. How does this act give Jesus' followers a powerful new memory aid of God's deliverance?

9. Just as the woman "broke and poured" the perfume Jesus does the same with the bread and cup, and (later) with His life. How does this sequence of events shed more light on the woman's initial act?

10. What is the significance of Jesus' death for people who see it as a beautiful act rather than a tragic waste?

11. The message of the Gospels is that Jesus took the condemnation we deserve upon Himself. What about Jesus' death has made the greatest impression on your life? Why?

12. What have you found in your study of Jesus to be of challenge or encouragement?

For Further Reflection

✦ The intention behind *Knowing Jesus* has been to fulfill the title by listening to the accounts of four men who knew Him well themselves. Their testimony reveals that Jesus stands in bold contrast to any would-be deity: *He is the Lord who would be our Servant.* And as the Servant Lord, He challenges those He meets to acknowledge His Lordship by humbly allowing Him to serve them.

Take some time to review this guide and write down some new discoveries you've made regarding Jesus' service to you. Consider using the following question to evaluate an issue or decision you are facing: *Given my options with this particular issue or decision, which choice do I expect would give Jesus the greatest opportunity to serve me?*

✦ Jesus will be able to serve us most in situations where we take appropriate risks. As we move out of our comfort zones and into the midst of other people's needs, He will be pleased to increasingly give us what we lack. And, of course, as we see our needs met by Him, like any servant, He will receive all the praise.

Notes for Leaders

Preparation

Begin your preparation with prayer and personal study. Prepare to lead your particular lesson by following the ten steps under *Suggestions for Personal Study* beginning on page 10.

Study the biblical context of the passage under consideration. Research any questions likely to sidetrack your group.

Study the flow of questions. TruthSeed questions are designed to create a flow of discussion from beginning to end. Get comfortable with the potential directions of the study. Mark pacing notes so that the discussion will spread evenly over your allotted time. Most TruthSeed studies should last about an hour.

Read the leader's notes for your particular study beginning on page 80. Mark information that you may need during the course of the study in the blank spaces of your question list.

If your group time includes other ingredients such as refreshments, music, worship, sharing, and prayer, plan time divisions so that your group is able to accomplish all that is scheduled. Many TruthSeed lessons make suggestions for these additional ingredients at the close of the Bible study section.

Acknowledge to yourself and to God that the group belongs to the people in it, not to you as a leader. TruthSeed is designed to facilitate a group discovery form of learning moderated by a discussion leader. Plan to lead with the group's welfare and interests in mind.

Pray for each group member by name.

Group Time

Begin on time. No apology necessary. The group has come together for a particular purpose and has assigned you the job of leading it in the study.

If your group is meeting for the first time, survey together the suggestions for group discussion on page 9. This will help each person to know what is expected and will get you off on a common footing.

Take appropriate note of the narrative introduction at the beginning of the study, then ask the opening question. Encourage responses from each person. When everyone seems involved in the subject at hand, the group will be ready to enter the biblical text. Since the opening questions point toward the text but do not interact with it, always ask the opening question BEFORE reading the Scripture.

Read the assigned Scripture passage aloud. Or ask several group members to read. Some people feel embarrassed about their reading skills, so don't make surprise assignments unless you are certain that they will be well accepted. Paragraph breaks in the text mark natural thought divisions, so always read by paragraphs, not by verses.

Conduct a discussion of the biblical text using the questions supplied. TruthSeed questions should promote multiple answers and group interaction. Allow time for several people to respond to each question and to each other. If the group does not seem to understand a particular question, rephrase it until it becomes clear, break it into smaller units, or give a brief summary and move on.

Give encouraging comments. If an answer is partially right, acknowledge that part. If an answer seems inappropriate, say something like, "What verse led you to that conclusion?" or "What do some of the rest of you think?"

Don't be afraid of silence. Help group members to become comfortable with the quiet by announcing a "thinking time." Then invite them to share their thoughtful responses to the questions at hand. Learn a sensitivity to God that can come from occasional silence.

Pace the study. It is the leader's responsibility to be sure that you finish on time and that the group has adequate time to discuss later questions. Some questions will take longer than others, so create a flexible pace with one eye on the clock and the other on interests of your group. Don't be afraid to redirect attention to the question list or the biblical text. Suggest that you may come back to some interesting topic after you have finished the study.

Involve everyone — more or less equally. Draw in quiet people by asking for nonthreatening opinion responses. Avoid direct eye contact with someone who talks a bit too much. If necessary, point out the shared responsibility for a successful discussion by reading item four on page 9.

Avoid over-talking yourself. Groups with an overactive leader get tempted to sit back and let the leader do *all* the work. Eventually, this causes people to lose the benefit of a personal encounter with the Scripture as it impacts their own lives.

Keep the discussion on track. Consider writing the purpose statement from the leader's section at the top of your question page so that you can keep the discussion objective in mind. You can head off a tangent by gently directing attention back to the biblical text. But do consider the relative merit of any potential tangent. Sometimes apparent tangents represent real needs that the group ought to address. In that case, adjust your plan (for the moment) and follow the needs of the group. If the tangent seems of limited interest or importance, offer to talk about it in more detail at a later time. Or if the tangent is of great importance, but requires further preparation, ask the group to table it for this session, but come back to it at a later meeting.

Don't skip questions of personal application. Here is where Scripture does its most important work. As other group members respond, be ready to add your own experiences of God's work in your life.

Open and close your study with prayer. Or ask someone in your group to do so.

Study One
Having Our Thirst Quenched
John 4:1-26

Purpose: To take Jesus up on His offer to fill our life with satisfaction and meaning.

Before You Begin. If the group is newly formed or if there are new members present, have people introduce themselves to each other. Feel free to let the group know, too, that you are not a teacher but a facilitator of discussion and that their contributions are critical for the success of the group.

Knowing Jesus: Our Lord, Our Servant is broken into four sections, each introduced with a brief description of that particular Gospel. Make sure you are familiar with *The Message of John* (p. 16) and let the group know how the series will progress with three studies in each Gospel.

You may find it educational and fun to introduce each section (starting with studies 1, 4, 7, and 10) to the group in a creative way. For instance, have someone give a 2–3 minute report he or she prepared ahead of time on the particular Gospel you are about to study. In one way or another, seek to apply some creative imagination with this.

Question 1. This first question should help the group break the ice and begin to relate more personally with each other concerning a central issue in the passage. If you feel the group can handle personalizing the question, you can ask: *What is something that disappoints you about your own life?*

Question 2. Help the group realize that this is an encounter that just should not have taken place — given conventions of their society (see v. 9). The contrast between the two could not be greater. Jesus is a respected Jewish Rabbi, and she is a Samaritan woman of questionable moral character. But meeting real needs is of primary importance to Jesus. Ethnic, gender, and spiritual prejudices will not deter Him.

Question 3. Encourage the group to "get to know" this woman as much as possible. If helpful, direct them to verse 17 and details of her life that it reveals.

Question 4. No typical Jew would have risked defilement by using a Samaritan woman's water utensil. But not only does Jesus engage her as an equal, He takes a position of weakness. If anyone was entitled to assume an elitist attitude, it was Jesus; instead He asks for her help in His request for a drink.

Use this question to discuss Jesus' model of ministry to people which begins at (or below!) their current level of understanding. A follow-up question would be: *What difference does it make to someone when we genuinely need their assistance?*

Question 5. The encounter began with Jesus requesting water from the woman (v. 7), but it doesn't take long before she ends up requesting a kind of water from Him (v. 15). Even so, her comprehension is narrow. Like Nicodemus, who took the new birth literally (3:4), she initially saw the offer of living water as a matter of convenience to cut down her work load!

This question should help the group understand her struggle to look beyond the physical realities of the gift that Jesus freely gives. He helps this woman see that indeed He is greater than her race's father Jacob whose well provides the context of their conversation (v. 12).

Later, Jesus again describes "living water." (See John 7:37-39.) There He identifies water with the Holy Spirit. The new life Jesus offers is as different from what the Samaritan woman has experienced as living water is from normal water. No wonder it is difficult for her to comprehend.

A reader gets the feeling that the woman asks her question of verse 12 with exasperation but it may well be her first step of faith. Her perspective is narrow and her reasoning is faulty, but at least her question is on target. In a fashion typical of Jesus, He did not give a direct answer but an ever-deepening disclosure of spiritual realities. Lead your group to come to these or similar conclusions.

Question 6. The woman's struggle with Jesus and the life He offers should give the group an opening to talk about their own initial encounter with Jesus.

Question 7. The transition between verses 15 and 16 from living water to the woman's personal life is rather startling. This may very well be Jesus' intention — so that she will begin to take Him seriously. His probing quickly touches an open wound in her life. His intimate knowledge of her takes her back and her defenses begin to unravel.

Question 8. This question should raise the issue of how people search for personal fulfillment. It is ultimately meant to lead the group toward identifying their own thirst as they respond to question 12.

Questions 9–11. Jesus is a master conversationalist. He provides a model for drawing people into talking about deep spiritual issues and their own personal lives. These questions should help the group appreciate Jesus and His style. As difficult as it can be, it is certainly worth opening our lives to His penetrating analysis and following His prescription to gain life.

Question 12. If this is your first meeting it might be best to stay together as a group to discuss this application. Feel free, however, to go around the circle in order to give each person an opportunity to respond. Be careful to pace yourself so as not to go over your designated ending time.

Study Two
Getting Our Hunger Satisfied
John 4:27-42

Purpose: To recognize that embracing God's will in extending His love to others will become a great source of strength for us.

Question 1. Have fun with this question by encouraging group members to describe in detail what it is that "gives them energy."

Question 2. This question refers to verse 27 as well as the rest of the chapter up to this point. There may be a person in your group who missed the first study. Even if not, it would be helpful to summarize the encounter of John 4:1-26. Ask the group for a volunteer to give a brief summary of the story and then fill in any details you feel are important. Emphasize the offer of living water that Jesus extends to the woman and the insights your group came up with in its previous study. However you handle this summation, keep it brief and intriguing.

Questions 3–4. The disciples suffer from the same narrow perspective previously seen in both Nicodemus (3:4) and the woman (4:11). They cannot see the connection between spiritual realities that are illustrated by the physical realm. So Jesus uses this occasion to teach them about the kind of food that satisfies and sustains.

Question 5. This is a key question so feel free to spend adequate time discussing it. Like living water that replenishes the spirit there is "living food" that sustains the soul. Many diverse pursuits can energize and motivate us. Jesus, however, wants us to evaluate them in the light of kingdom values. Real satisfaction comes as our "small ambitions" find fulfillment in the Great Ambition of pursuing the work of God in the lives of people. The food that sustained Jesus came from the sure knowledge that in reaching out to this woman He was doing the will and work of the One who sent Him.

Question 6. Our food source is the same as what Jesus describes for Himself. While it was natural for Jesus to look to His Father to guide His ministry, it is not so natural for us. This question highlights our struggle to find sustenance through involvement in the work of God on behalf of people rather than in other pursuits.

Question 7. This section presents some difficulty because we do not know exactly to what the quote in verse 35 refers. Is it a familiar proverb to the disciples, or a chance remark as they looked at the fields green with crops in the early stage of growth, or something else? Either way, the emphasis is one of urgency.

Jesus' repetition of "even now" (v. 36) highlights the eager activity of the reaper with the underlying call for His disciples to have the same eagerness. The "others" who have done the hard work (v. 38) may be a reference to the Old Testament prophets, John the Baptist, the woman (see v. 39-42), and/or Jesus Himself. Again, to whomever it may refer, the disciples now have the rare privilege to experience the joy of reaping without the hard work of sowing. What could be better!?!

Questions 8–9. The woman's exciting discovery that Jesus is "living water" finds her energized by the "living food" which doing His will and work provides. Jesus has become her water and her bread. And so, apparently, has He for many in her town. Help your group sense the great joy of this event. Feel free to unleash a little imagination with a follow-up question such as: *What difference do you imagine the town people's experience with Jesus would make in their relationships with each other?*

Question 11. Encourage your group to be as specific as possible with this question. Feel free to ask: *Could you give a specific example of that?* to help illustrate their answers. Also if time permits, you could go around the circle so that each group member has an opportunity to share. Or break up into groups of 3–4 for sharing and prayer.

For Further Reflection: You could make this a "group project." If you make these plans together, follow up at your next meeting so that people can report on how they carried out their intentions—and the results.

Study Three

Letting Jesus Wash Our Feet

John 13:1-17

Purpose: To grow in our appreciation of Jesus' service on our behalf.

Question 1. Most often the message people come away with from their study of John 13:1-17 is the need to serve others. While this is an emphasis, especially in verses 14-17, it is in fact secondary and an outcome of the primary focus: the need to allow Jesus to serve us.

This study highlights the critical issue of being willing recipients. The first question should help the group get a feel for how difficult it is to be on the receiving end.

Question 2. If the group does not take note of the verbs, point them out. These verbs help give the impression of a very deliberate act on Jesus' part. Be sure to draw from the whole passage.

Question 4. As Jesus circled the table washing feet—an act considered so humble it was not even required of Jewish slaves—Peter must have squirmed at the awkward role reversal. He probably thought that he himself or one of the other disciples should have taken up the towel and basin and washed Jesus' feet instead. Help the group to get a "feel" for Peter's consternation.

Question 5. Jesus would have none of Peter's role reversal. "Unless I wash you," replied Jesus, "you have no part with me (v. 8)." The act of foot washing foreshadowed Jesus' death on the cross the very next day. In a small way Jesus illustrated for Peter his need to receive. As a rhetorical question you might ask: *If Peter could not receive this small act of servanthood, how would he be prepared to receive the much greater act of Jesus' sacrifice for sin?*

Question 6. This is the key issue in the passage, and yet some in your group may disagree with the direction this question takes, so let me elaborate here. Regarding who serves whom, Jesus will only relate to us as the One who serves. Peter never got the chance to wash Jesus' feet because "the Son of Man did not come to be served but to serve" (Mark 10:45).

Consider these concepts drawn from *Desiring God* by John Piper: Jesus said we cannot serve both God and money (Matthew 6:24). How would we serve money? Certainly not by assisting it or helping it, but by believing money will provide for our happiness and welfare. *To serve God, then, is to recognize His superior trustworthiness and believe that He will provide for our happiness and welfare.*

This is not a matter of fine tuning our relationship with God. For their work, employees get their due wages—not a gift. But our life with God hangs on the very fact that we *don't* get what is coming to us. God is the workman, the employee. Our "work," if you can call it that, is to exercise faith by receiving His work—the gift of grace (John 6:29).

In their legalistic, religious zeal, many of Jesus' contemporaries had given in to a view of God as a recipient of human effort. Jesus offers Peter—not a change in degree but a change in kind. Understanding that it is God who serves us is at the heart of our relationship to God. It separates Christianity from every other religion.

Question 7. Some first-century Christians objected to the idea that Jesus *alone* stood at the heart of one's spirituality. They tended to add something—like Jesus plus some secret knowledge, or Jesus plus some Jewish laws—to "round out" their relationship with God. John is countering gnostic influence in the church and possibly the Judaizers as well. There is just nothing we can add to Jesus' service to us . . . but that is all we need. Peter's raises the same issue, wondering if something more than Jesus' servanthood was needed. If time permits, you might want to add the question: *What are you most tempted to add to Jesus' service for you even though it is not fundamental to knowing Him?*

Question 8. When Jesus does make the call to follow His example, He does so in a way made even more dramatic in retrospect. In His case, servanthood included washing someone's feet—Peter's, who would within hours deny Him, and another's—Judas', who would betray Him to his enemies for crucifixion.

Question 9. If your group struggles with this concept, think of an example to use in the discussion such as one or both of the following. It is ludicrous for a patron at a restaurant to boast about how well he was allowing the waiter to serve him or for a hospital patient to boast about how well she was following the doctor's prescription to get well.

Taking pride in being served by Jesus is just as inappropriate because our discipleship is the means of *us* being blessed and getting healed. As our Lord, Jesus doesn't want our work but our willingness. And as our Servant, He does not warrant our pride but our praise.

Question 10. Both the desire and the ability to love others, especially when it comes to loving our worst enemies, comes from an ongoing experience of being loved. If we are not letting Jesus wash our feet, there will be no supernatural power—the ingredient necessary for finding joy in the washing of others' feet.

For Further Reflection. This study is key to the entire study guide. So encourage your group to reflect this week on the significance of seeing God as our servant and reflecting on the way He serves us.

Study Four
Receiving a Change of Vocation
Luke 5:1-11

Purpose: To discover Jesus' overriding vocation for His people.

Introduction. Remind the group of the progression of this series. The studies in John have focused on receiving from Jesus. The three studies in Luke will help us see the challenge His service to us brings to our lives.

Question 1. Have fun with this question by telling people to let their imaginations run wild. This is to be their "dream job" and that doesn't mean it pays very well or even pays at all. You could ask a follow-up question like: *Who is the person in this world who has the best job you can imagine?*

Question 2. Help the group get a firsthand "feel" for the scene. What does it look like? Smell like? This is a first-century fresh fish market—but apparently with no fish on this day! While Peter & Co. clean their nets, tired and frustrated from a fruitless night of fishing, others are crowding around to hear an itinerant preacher explain God's Word.

Question 3. Jesus' first request to Peter in verse 3 (to use his boat for teaching) and his second request in verse 4 (to go out to the deep water) are not their first encounter. As a matter of fact, this particular call of the disciples comes after John, Andrew, Peter, and others' first meeting with Jesus (recorded in John 1:35-51) and after their initial call (recorded in Mark 1:16-20 and Matthew 4:18-22). Apparently they had joined Jesus before and yet continued with their family's fishing business. Now the call of Jesus was going to demand their full-time attention.

Question 4. This question is meant to help your group see the almost humorous and certainly awkward position in which Jesus' request placed Peter. Here was a carpenter, turned healer and preacher, telling a seasoned fisherman how to carry on his trade. Peter's initial protestation is certainly understandable. He knew that now during the heat of midday was the *wrong time* to fish and that outside the shallows in the deep water was the *wrong place* to fish. Besides, having come up empty themselves, they had just finished cleaning their nets!

Question 5. The catch of fish is utterly astounding even to the point of sinking two boats (v. 7). You could stir things up by asking the group: *Why didn't Peter's business instincts motivate him to proposition Jesus as the newest, and obviously most effective, partner in their Galilean fishing business? "You and me, Jesus. We'd make a great team!"*

Of course nothing of the kind happens. Instead, Peter's reaction is to send Jesus away. Another way to ask the second question is: *What does sin have to do with fish? Why does Peter react to the catch so strongly?*

Question 6. Peter's reaction comes from a twofold realization. First, he now more fully understands that Jesus is no ordinary Rabbi with beginner's luck. He is not just a "Master" (v. 5) who is worthy of respect but the "Lord" (v. 8) who deserves full-time and unreserved commitment. Peter simultaneously realizes his own unworthiness of Jesus' presence: "Go away from me, Lord; I am a sinful man." (For a similar Old Testament example of such an encounter with God see Isaiah 6:1-8.)

Question 7. Before you ask question 7 it could be helpful to direct the group back to Luke 4:38-44 and ask: *How has Peter seen Jesus up to this point?* For Peter has heard Jesus speak and not been so moved, and he has even seen Jesus heal his mother-in-law (v. 38) and not been so moved.

But now Jesus' presence is "up-front and personal." The focus is on a central issue of Peter's life: his vocation. If there is one thing that he understands and has under control, it is his fishing business. But the expert turns novice when the master fisherman shows up. No longer is fishing an area where Peter can claim a sense of mastery. The carpenter from Nazareth is Lord, even of his fishing business.

Questions 8–9. Whereas Jesus' Lordship is the central issue, *fear* is the central emotion in this story, and you should not let the group pass over this key ingredient too quickly. It is a fearsome thing to see God for who He is and to see ourselves for who we are. Jesus does not let Peter's fear become debilitating but uses it as a turning point in their relationship. And as these disciples enter into full-time commitment, they bequeath to their families one huge catch of fish that will likely take care of their needs for some time to come!

Question 10. This question is meant to help the group see that Jesus takes a person where he is and helps him take the steps of commitment in a reasonable way. In this encounter Jesus helps Peter & Co. trust Him to make greater commitments as He slowly but surely ups the ante of His requests. First He asks Peter for the use of his boat for teaching (v. 3) and then to put out into deep water to let his nets down for a catch (v. 4). Now, after Peter has repeatedly seen Jesus come through for him, Jesus challenges Peter to commit himself in a wholehearted way (v. 10) and leave his fishing business in order to partner with Jesus. Jesus' Lordship demands all, but not in a demanding way.

For Further Reflection. If time allows, this section can be integrated into the study between questions 10 and 11. Otherwise use it for personal follow-up after the study. If your group is inclined toward journaling, suggest a five-minute quiet time while they write a response to this section. Then use these "journal entries" as springboards for discussion that leads into question 11. If time is short, suggest that some time before the next meeting, they write a letter to God about their reflections on this section. Those who are willing may then read their letters aloud at your next meeting.

Study Five
Sitting at Jesus' Feet
Luke 10:25-42

Purpose: To realize that the greatest priority in life is not to serve Jesus but to "sit at His feet."

Question 1. You may find it helpful to go around the circle on this question in order to get each person involved in the discussion from the onset.

Question 2. As was His custom, (see Luke 9:52) Jesus likely sent word ahead of His visit. Although Lazarus is not mentioned here, John notes that three siblings — Martha, Mary, and Lazarus — shared this Bethany home (John 11:1).

Question 3. Very likely Martha is the older sister since Luke refers to "her home" (v. 38), and consequently Martha assumes responsibility that everything would be just right for Jesus' visit. And you can bet Martha was not about to treat these visitors to a cold-cuts affair. It was time to get out the best china, use the sterling silver, and spread the kind of dinner fit for such a Guest. With determination and dedication she fired up the oven, put on her apron, and started the preparation.

Questions 4–5. Help your group get a feel for Martha's frustration. Things come unglued for her when her younger sister Mary fails to check in as an assistant. And to make matters worse, Mary appears to suffer from a complete mental lapse as to the proper role of women in her day and age! With potatoes unpeeled, bread unbaked, and the table unset, she sits in the living room with the other disciples listening to Jesus.

You might want to give the group an even greater feel for Martha's situation with a question such as: *Have you ever been left with a sink full of dishes while other family members slip out to the TV room?* (And have you ever slipped into the TV room and left the dishes?!) *What did you feel like when you were left with no help?* Martha feels the same way: jilted, resentful, angry.

Question 7. Have fun with this. Repeat good responses and even take a vote in your group for the most accurate one!

Question 8. The critical observation your group should see is the contrast between Martha and Mary. Martha's problem is, in a word, priorities: doing the good and missing the best. Jesus, though appreciative of her hospitality, wanted her attention and loyalty more than her roast beef and green beans. He came to her home not to be the object of her motherly affection so much as the Compassionate Host; not to be served but to serve (Mark 10:45).

Mary understood the priority of the moment and would not allow the pressure of social convention or even an older sister to sidetrack her. The "better thing" that she had chosen was being with Jesus.

Question 10. Martha's hostessing dilemma becomes even more apparent when her encounter with Jesus is seen in light of the preceding passage—the Parable of the Good Samaritan (Luke 10:25-37). In the Good Samaritan parable, Jesus answers a lawyer's question of "Who is my neighbor?" with a vivid illustration of hospitality.

If time is running short you can verbally describe the teaching of the Good Samaritan parable which simply put is: *Be hospitable to those in need.* Jesus ends the story with the words, "Go and do likewise."

Note that Luke then ties these two stories together, not chronologically but conceptually. Martha, starting in the very next verse (v. 38), does what Jesus had just told the lawyer to do: She assumes the role of the Good Samaritan and reaches out with hospitality. But Martha tried to apply the second command before the first. Love for neighbor falls short if it is not undergirded by love for God (Luke 10:27). Martha mistakenly thought that much serving added up to much spirituality. But according to the love chapter of 1 Corinthians 13, service from compulsion and not love is of no profit.

Question 11. This question is meant to help the group look into the mirror of reality. Martha had fallen into the "Christian activity trap" — serving Jesus, serving Jesus, serving Jesus — and yet failing to quietly sit at His feet. Some additional questions to ask to stimulate discussion would include: *Do you use the word "busy" a lot and yet sense that you're "running on empty" spiritually? Is your schedule characterized by event after event, including church meetings, that do not seem to add up to spiritual life? Explain.*

We identify with Martha because we often prefer to hang out in the kitchen where people are serving Jesus and avoid the living room where people are listening to Him. We'd rather help than hear, cook than commune, work than worship. Frankly, its much easier. *Kitchen Christianity* helps us feel useful and important. "It's a tough job but someone has to do it! Here I am Lord; use me."

Question 12. Jesus calls people to "be with Him" (Mark 3:14). Mary knows that the greatest priority is not to serve Jesus but to sit at His feet; discipleship is not fueled by compulsion or duty but by affection and devotion. Before her service in the kitchen for Jesus can be effective, her sitting in the living room is required.

Luke 10:38-42 does not so much contrast the life of service with the life of contemplation as much as it fosters *a way of service.* Since Jesus is God and thus has no needs, our service to Him takes the form of a willingness to listen and to learn. Such a process will produce the kind of hospitality which sees that Jesus is graciously meeting our needs even in the very act of our service to others.

For Further Reflection. *Test Your Drivenness.* You may want to give this test right after question 1 and then discuss it at the end of the study. Another option is to use it as a follow-up to the study.

Study Six
Spending Like There's No Tomorrow
Luke 19:11-27

Purpose: To discover the importance and benefits of taking risks in our life with God.

Question 1. You could precede this question with something like: *What was the most foolhardy, daredevil thing you did as a kid?* If you ask this first, however, follow it up by asking about a risk taken as an adult.

Question 2. The story of Zacchaeus (Luke 19:1-10) provides the backdrop for Jesus telling this parable. It would be helpful to summarize the story before discussing this question. To do this refer or even read the second half of the introduction of this study beginning with the paragraph: "Scripture is full of people who had guts. . . ."

Question 4. What the mina is can be interpreted differently. In its most narrow definition, it can be understood as the Gospel message which we have all been given and have the responsibility to spread. But it seems that a broader interpretation is in order here. The one thing we have all been given is *life.* How we invest what we have been given (whether it is the particular message of the Gospel or the whole of our life) is the question with which this parable confronts us.

Question 5. Your group should understand that the parable presents two options of what people can do with their mina—their life. One option is seen in the third servant's conservative, "be-very-careful" attitude to life which is drawn out in questions 7 and 8.

The other option is to take what we have and invest it as the first two servants did. Their life motto can be interpreted: "Nothing ventured, nothing gained." "Spend, spend, spend like there's no tomorrow!" You might want to think of an illustration of seemingly wild and imprudent spending to convey the attitude consistent with the actions of the first two servants.

The first servant came in with an amazing report (v. 16), "Sir, your mina has earned ten more." To this his master replied, "Well done, my good servant!" And you can see why; in percentage terms that servant earned a whopping 1000 percent on the king's money!

Help the group realize how unusual such a high return would be. You could ask them: *Where can you get 100 percent return on your money let alone 500–1000 percent?* Or relate a personal experience of a sour investment scheme.

These two servants must have put the King's money into some kind of high-risk venture to get that kind of return. It was wild and imprudent investing. This makes junk bonds look like iron-clad safe, FDIC-guaranteed investments! You might as well put your money in Siberian gold mines. To the financial community — especially in a pre-venture capitalist society — this is incredible, it's shocking, it's outrageous. And that is exactly Jesus' point in the parable.

So the parable is not about investing money but about what difference our view and relationship with God will make in how we live our lives. Believing that God will ultimately provide for us will not lead us to unwisely cancel insurance policies or empty savings accounts. But it will lead us to trust God rather than these or other things to take care of us. And if we know that He will take care of us, we are free to "abandon" ourselves in a hurting world where we can *spend* our lives for the sake of others.

Question 8. Begin this question by having someone read verses 20-21: "Sir, here is your mina; I have kept it laid away in a piece of cloth. I was afraid of you, because you are a hard man. You take out what you did not put in and reap what you did not sow."

The king in this parable represents the Lord. The third servant is a person who views God as a "hard man" who, if He ever really got hold of you, would squeeze all the juices out. God, in this view, is a tight, exacting man who carries a big stick and a long list of rules.

Help the group get into the mind-set of the third servant. Since the third servant does not really know the king or his ability to provide, he greatly fears the future and adopts a "save it for a rainy day" mentality. Each action in life is calculated and recalculated. Decisions and life values follow the safest, most protected path available. At least if the mina is buried in the ground, it will not be lost. . . . or will it?!!

Question 9. This is a general application question but is not meant to lead just to a philosophical discussion. It is critical to understand that our view of God will have a life-changing affect on the way we live our lives. Why? Because if we see ourselves as God's workman doing our duty for Him, then we will end up with the same view of God that the third servant had: That God is a hard man, a difficult boss trying to get as much out of us as He can. This is obligation faith which seeks to find out just what the rules are and then live by them or even exceed them as the Pharisees did.

Note that we might not *say* we view God as a hard man who uses us, but if we live our lives as the third servant did—by hording and protecting what we have—our actions betray our true feelings. We say, in effect, be careful, don't take risks—God cannot be trusted to take care of me.

You might find it appropriate to follow up this question by personalizing it: *How do you view God? In what ways do you sometimes view God in the same way as the third servant?*

Question 11. Make sure that your group sees taking risks as a serious act of commitment that bring consequences. People who invest themselves in the lives of others are often taken for granted or taken advantage of. It might even be helpful to ask for examples of this. (The introduction provides one such example.)

But the ultimate positive message here is that God can be trusted to come through when we step out of our prearranged script for our life. Whatever it is we hold too near and dear—our family, career, bank account, ambitions, future—we can learn to let go. "What would it profit a man," Jesus asked, "to gain the whole world"—to live out that prearranged script—"and forfeit his life. . . . Those who save their life, lose it but those who lose their life, save it." Spend, spend, spend, (our lives) like there's no tomorrow.

Question 12. If time permits, go around the circle so each person can respond. Or break into smaller groups to respond and pray.

For Further Reflection. Use this activity as a prayerful closing to your study. Or assign it for the week and come back to it when you open your next session.

Study Seven
Pursuing the Things Worthy of Pursuit
Matthew 16:13-28

Purpose: To recognize that in God's kingdom self-denial ultimately leads to self-benefit.

Introduction: Note the transition between studying Luke and now Matthew. The emphasis of Matthew's Gospel is learning from Jesus. These studies will help your group see how Jesus wants people to evaluate the costs and benefits of following Him and make decisions that are in their best long-term interest.

Question 1. After asking this question you could follow it up with: *Have you recently made a public statement that you later failed to carry through? If so, how did you feel?* The intention here is not to describe embarrassments but to identify the power of public announcements.

Question 2. In light of the religious leaders' view of Jesus, the particular opinion the disciples cite, that Jesus is a figure such as John the Baptist, Elijah or Jeremiah, is rather positive. But Jesus does not care so much about a positive opinion as an accurate one. So He takes this opportunity to get a reality check. Are His disciples—the ones who are constantly at His side and know Him best—figuring out just who He is? This dialogue provides a turning point in the relationship between Jesus and His disciples. They can never again consider themselves to be simply observers of this intriguing man from Nazareth.

Question 3. Peter's announcement of who Jesus is prompts Jesus' declaration of who Peter is. Note, as the footnote of the NIV translation indicates, the Greek word *Peter* is also the word for *rock*. So Jesus' declaration is: "You are Peter (rock) and on this rock I will build my church . . ." (v. 18).

The interpretation of this verse and the ones that follow have varied widely. Some consider Peter's confession of the Gospel message, "you are the Christ" as the "rock" upon which the church is established. Many, however, understand the passage as a confirmation of Peter as the spiritual leader of the church. Roman Catholics have developed their belief of papal succession from Jesus' choice of Peter as the church's leader—"the first pope." Other commentators, while agreeing that Jesus is confirming the leadership of Peter among the apostles, do not believe Jesus is setting up a succession of spiritual authority which must then be passed on from one worldwide leader (pope) to the next.

Feel free to let your group discuss this and even agree to disagree if necessary. Just encourage them to stay within the passage's context for the discussion. One other issue to note are the words "be bound" and "be loosed" (v. 19) which in rabbinical terms means *forbidding* and *permitting.*

Question 4. The Greek term "Christ" refers to *the anointed* and translates the Hebrew term "Messiah." Throughout the centuries Jewish messianic speculation was linked to and overshadowed by aspirations to be free from Gentile domination. In their yearning to be politically free from Roman rule, most people of Jesus' day would have difficultly equating the triumph of God's kingdom coming in the person of a suffering Messiah. Peter shares this difficulty, but for him the idea that Jesus would suffer strikes a personal chord, and he seeks to change Jesus' intentions.

Questions 5–6. Give the group adequate time to discuss why Jesus is so sharp in His rebuke of Peter. Peter's insistence on setting Jesus' agenda leads naturally into a discussion concerning our own tendency to do the same.

Question 8. The purpose of denying ourself is often misunderstood. Getting out of bed in the morning is a matter of self-denial for many of us! But this act of self-discipline brings the reward of a productive life and that's why we fight off the "pad monster."

Denying ourself, from Jesus' perspective, is not an end in itself but a means to an end of saving ourself. It could then be said that self-denying is the most self-benefiting thing one could do! Feel free to ask the group for some specific examples of how self-denial, though it may lead to great hardship, will also result in self-benefit.

Question 9. The Cross provides our greatest point of identification with Jesus. For it is on our account that He "must suffer." Taking up our cross amounts to renouncing any attempt of prudent self-reliant or self-justifying behavior. It commits us to follow the path to glory that Jesus chose. On that path, we humbly embrace God's will and ways—no matter what the consequences. Encourage your group to be as personal and specific as is appropriate.

Question 10. Some people are uncomfortable with the idea that self-benefit is something to be pursued. But Jesus seems to at least acknowledge, if not encourage it, by giving us the recipe in this passage: "For whoever wants to save his life will lose it, but whoever loses his life for me will find it."

It may foster a helpful discussion to ask: *Is there a difference between selfishness and self-interestedness? If so, what would it be?*

It could be argued that while selfishness seeks its own sinful ends through manipulating others to meet its needs, true self-interest seeks the benefits of God's blessing through losing one's life for the sake of others. This is a strange kind of self-interest but is at the very heart of the Gospel's paradox that those who lose their life find it.

For Further Reflection. You might want to make this a "group project." If so follow up on how it went at your next group meeting.

Study Eight
Coming Down off the Mountaintop
Matthew 17:1-20

Purpose: To see that dependence on God can help us deal with both the highs and lows life brings our way.

Question 1. Encourage the group to be specific with this. Consider speaking first in order to model the kind of sharing you desire.

Question 2. The passage for today's study comes directly after the passage for study 7. As such, it may be helpful to summarize the events of Matthew 16:13-28 before reading today's text aloud.

Question 3. Obviously Peter's mouth is running ahead of his mind. Feel free to have some fun with this question in your group. You could even speculate as to what he meant!

Question 4. These questions are meant to compare and contrast Jesus with these key spokesmen of the Old Testament.

Question 5. You might want to preface this question with the following: There are at least five possible events that would fulfill Jesus' prediction in Matthew 16:28 — the Transfiguration, Resurrection, Ascension, the Day of Pentecost or the Second Coming of Christ. The Second Coming does not seem to fit with the fact that all those Jesus spoke to would not die before it takes place. All the other events, however, anticipate the glory of Jesus fully revealed through the Second Coming.

Question 6. The teachers of the Law mistakenly looked for the literal return of Elijah as the forerunner of Messiah's coming. According to Jesus, John the Baptist fulfilled the prophecy. The effects of John's ministry — seen in the repentance of his listeners — fulfilled the restoration Malachi spoke about in Malachi 4:5-6. The people as a whole, however, failed to recognize John as the one who would prepare the way. (See Matthew 11:16-18.) Instead of consulting the Lord as to what to do with John, Jesus said that they did "everything they wished" (17:12).

Question 7. The words from the voice in heaven are identical to those spoken at Jesus' baptism: "This is my Son, whom I love; with Him I am well pleased." (See also Matthew 3:17.) Now, however, a command is added: "Listen to Him." This has direct application, especially now that the disciples have come to recognize Jesus for who He is. Luke quotes Jesus as saying, "From everyone who has been given much, much will be demanded" (12:48).

Question 8. Jesus' rebuke was directed to an "unbelieving and perverse generation." This applies to a greater or lesser extent to all present including the scribes, crowd, father, and the nine disciples unable to heal the boy. (The father, however, at least had enough faith to bring his son in the first place.) In contrast to the experience of the Transfiguration, the pitiful state of unbelief Jesus now confronts is left for the reader to contemplate.

The disciples themselves may have been quite surprised that they lacked the power of healing. Hadn't they, not long before, exercised the power of Jesus and healed many? You might want to ask: *What has happened in the meantime?* Apparently their faithlessness comes in the form of a presumptuous faith, which is not genuine faith at all.

Question 9. A mustard seed, in proverbial Jewish thinking, was considered the smallest of seeds in Jesus' day. Though it is tiny it is the genuine article which is verified by the tree-sized shrub it produces. This seed of faith can move mountains because it humbly places its dependence on the power and resources of God.

Questions 10–11. There are three applications beginning here that may lead to helpful discussion. Be careful to manage your time carefully. Consider breaking the group into twos or threes and ask the groups to respond to the two parts of question ten. Then, if time allows, bring the whole group back together and go around the circle so each person can respond to question 11. After this you can again break into small groups to end in prayer.

Study Nine
Counting the Costs and the Benefits
Matthew 19:13-30

Purpose: To understand that the desire to follow Jesus comes from realizing that the benefits outweigh the costs.

Question 1. The purpose of this question is to get a feel for how attached we are to the things we own. Go around the circle so each can share. Encourage the group to be honest. A little humor here wouldn't hurt either!

Questions 2–3. The reason to include verses 13-15 is to see the contrast between the disciples' values and Jesus' values regarding those they encounter. In most societies, including the one Jesus lived in, children have little or no status. Jesus' love for children comes through loud and clear. For additional information, you can compare the events here with Matthew 18:1-6.

The young rich man naturally commanded respect. Beyond his wealth he apparently was a religious person interested in spiritual things. Jesus' value system involves extending kindness and hospitality to the most (and also to the least) important members of society.

Question 5. Jesus does not ask the man if he has kept the "vertical commandments" related to loving God. Maybe He held back, anticipating the smug, superficial response He would receive: "All these I have kept. What do I still lack?" Whatever the reason, Jesus' challenge cuts through the veil of virtue and respectability to address the man's ongoing spiritual anxiety. Your group should come to these or similar conclusions.

Question 6. A good follow-up to the second part may be: *Is Jesus' challenge unduly harsh?* In requiring the man to sell and give away his possessions, Jesus seeks to help the man find what he lacks. Fundamentally, what he lacks is the inclination to trust Jesus to take care of him. I expect Jesus would have even been satisfied if the man had confessed his idolatry and asked Jesus if he could continue to stay on with Him where he could learn of God's trustworthiness. Money was a secondary issue.

But what Jesus demanded of the man was appropriate to the situation. He does not ask every rich person (for example Joseph of Arimathea in Matthew 27:57) to do the same. He does, however, search out our "hidden" idolatries, whatever they may be, and calls us to place our full trust in Him.

Questions 8–9. Because the rich man's problem is so often our own, the application question focuses on possessions. Feel free to go around the circle and have each person mention a response to question 9.

Note that although Jesus appeals to the benefits, He *never* includes wealth as one of these benefits as do the modern proponents of "prosperity gospel." More likely, as was true for the rich young man, we will need to forsake the pursuit of wealth to receive the greater riches inherited in a dependent relationship to God. But taking Jesus up on this deal—and that's exactly what He offers this first-century businessman—is definitely in our best interest. We'd be fools to count treasure on earth as worth more than treasure in heaven.

Questions 10–11. Some in your group may be uncomfortable with Peter's bottom-line question, but Jesus does not seem taken aback by it. Instead he appears to make a blatant appeal to self-interest. A follow-up question would be: *Why according to verse 29 should we follow Jesus?*

Question 12. The intention in these final application questions is to highlight the contrasting motivation from *duty*—because we have to—versus *desire*—because we want to. God does not want our dutiful obedience any more than a wife or girlfriend wants dutiful flowers.

Study Ten
Managing Our Time, Jesus' Style
Mark 1:21-45

Purpose: To learn from a great example of how to choose the best over the good.

Introduction: Mark's Gospel provides the passages for the last three studies. We will focus on our response to Jesus' call which involves us with Him in the work of the kingdom.

Question 1. Urgent demands may include legitimate concerns, but they may also intrude on our life to steal away time and energy that could be better spent. As it has been said, "The enemy of the best is the good." It might be helpful to have your group list urgent demands and important priorities. Busywork, interruptions, and some phone calls could be examples of the first while long-range planning, prayer, exercise, and relationships might be examples of the latter.

Questions 2–4. Point out to the group that Mark 1:21-34 appears to be a single day in Jesus' life and in this case a Sabbath day. These questions should help your group get a feel for the wide variety of challenges Jesus faced in a typical day. Keep the pace moving through verses 21-34 in order to give enough time to the section that follows.

Verses 21-22 compare Jesus' teaching with that of the teachers of the law. While these teachers were careful to teach by precedent — basing their authority on previously established interpretations — Jesus based His authority on His own judgment.

Verses 23-28 describe a confrontation with evil spirits who had taken possession of a man. Their acknowledgment of His identity is not a confession but an attempt to gain advantage over Him. The same authority seen in Jesus' teaching is now demonstrated in his simple word to the spirits: "Be quiet! Come out of him!"

In the previous verses, Jesus has demonstrated His authority over truth and over the spirit realm. He now turns toward physical illness. Verses 29-31 describe a straightforward, unpretentious display of Jesus' control in the healing of Simon's mother-in-law. Then, as if this day hadn't been full enough, Jesus continued His work of healing and exercising demons late into the night. (See vv. 32-34.) Your group should make these or similar observations about the information in the text.

Question 5. Your group should realize that Jesus' early morning commitment to prayer comes after an extremely hard day and night of work. The fascinating thing, however, is not just His commitment to prayer but the influence that this particular prayer had on His life. (This becomes apparent later in the text.) For now your group should note that Jesus was just as tempted as we are to allow the urgent demands of life to encroach on truly important concerns. Jesus knew that private time with the Father made the difference between going along with the flow and taking control of it.

Question 6. Help group members to be as specific as possible in describing their feelings about their own prayer lives by asking for personal illustrations. There may be a tendency to just recount frustrations so encourage people to describe successes in their prayer practices as well.

Questions 7–8. Peter assumes the role of Jesus' handler and has incorporated the crowd's agenda into setting out Jesus' schedule. The crowd wanted Jesus-the-miracle-worker. And what a temptation for Him — steady work, adoring fans, little or no flak, a ready outlet for compassion, a lot of excitement.

But in order to give time to the best things, Jesus takes away time from the good things. His dedication to prayer came partly from realizing that prayer gave Him more time, not less. It helped crystallize the important priorities and dissipate the merely urgent ones. While we may never fully understand how prayer affects God or adds power to the outworking of His intentions, we do know that the practice of prayer helps us.

Guide your group into a discussion that highlights how the pressure from Peter and the crowd opposes the Father's perspective. A follow-up question would be: *How would time spent with His Father give Jesus the strength to resist urgent pressures to concentrate on important priorities?*

Question 9. Verse 38 is key to understanding the heart of Jesus' vision for ministry, so feel free to extend the group discussion concerning this verse. Surely preaching is a more mundane task than working acts of miracles. But in saying "no" to the good Jesus is able to say "yes" to the best.

Questions 10–11. Try to pace the study in a way that gives the group plenty of time to address these application questions. If helpful, have each person respond to these questions by going around the circle.

Question 12. The tendency will be for everyone to identify spending time in prayer and Bible study. This is certainly applicable but press the group for other specific applications as well. If time allows go around in the circle so each can answer or divide into groups of 3 or 4 to share and pray.

Study Eleven
Giving Others Something to Eat
Mark 6:6b-13, 30-44

Purpose: To trust God that He will take care of us as we put others and their needs first.

Question 1. It would be helpful to personalize this question and ask your group members to illustrate a recent experience in which they felt stretched beyond their limit and what they did to try to cope.

Questions 2–3. Your group should recognize that Jesus' instructions are not meant to establish permanent criteria for the church. They are relevant for this particular situation and provide some general principles of ministry.

Dividing the groups into pairs fulfills the Old Testament emphasis "on the testimony of two or three witnesses" (Numbers 35:30; Deuteronomy 17:6). The instructions to not leave the first house they are invited into (v. 10) would keep them from dishonoring their host by moving to more comfortable housing. Opposition will also come, and the response to "shake the dust off your feet" (v. 11) provides a sobering symbolic warning that one's link to the truth of the Gospel depends not only on the listeners but on the messengers as well. It also encourages the messengers not to brood over past failures but to continue their work in new territory.

Jesus' restrictions put the disciples into a "survival mode" in which they must depend on God and others to provide for their most basic needs. Such dependence will give their ministry the greatest possible opportunity for success. Being dependent makes the disciples humble recipients. Their authority comes from their willingness to receive. Any temptation to abuse power dissolves in the reality of their need to ask the very people they are ministering to for food and shelter. People who feel needed are more likely to listen.

Question 5. Feel free to spend plenty of time focusing on the contrast between the attitudes of Jesus and the disciples. It is a key issue in the passage. A good follow-up question would be: *Are people a hindrance to you or are they tremendously important and worthy of attention?* The disciples want to "send the people away" (v. 36), but Jesus sees them "like sheep without a shepherd" (v. 34).

The disciples are likely disappointed that the opportunity for debriefing after their ministry experience has been shut down by the needs of people, but that is just the point. People's needs have become the essence of their call and if they feel overwhelmed, then their earlier lesson of what it means to depend on God must now be taken even more seriously. Your group should make similar observations from study of the text.

Question 6. For most of Jesus' miracles the disciples are passive observers. Not so here. Jesus draws them into the "grocery dilemma" in order to reinforce what it means to minister in His name.

Question 8. The disciples' response appears to be sarcastic, but (from a human point of view) who can blame them? An interesting follow-up question would be: *How do you imagine you would have responded?*

Question 9. If helpful, have someone in the group summarize Jesus' instructions in verses 8-11 and what these restrictions were meant to encourage. What seems apparent in both situations is that effectiveness in ministry is directly tied to dependence on God.

Question 10. You might want to note for the group the vivid language of verses 39-44 (for example the green grass of verse 39). The description here draws on Old Testament imagery in which God provides for His people as a shepherd cares for his sheep. (See Psalm 23 and Ezekiel 34.)

Question 12. Encourage the group to be specific here. *Can you give a specific example of that?* may be a good follow-up question to vague answers of application. If appropriate have the group break into groups of 3 or 4 to talk and pray over this question.

Study Twelve
Having Something to Remember
Mark 14:1-26

Purpose: To remind ourselves of Jesus' remarkable provision on our behalf.

Question 1. Childhood memories may be a touchy subject for some in your group, but this question is meant to raise very positive ones. Encourage members to describe what gave and continues to give them joy concerning these memories. An alternative question which you could use is: *What is an object you have which reminds you of a positive event or activity from your childhood?*

Question 2. This question is meant to not only highlight the diverse cast of characters but to give the group some broad observations of the passage. A follow-up question could ask: *What different motives are present in the people involved?*

Question 3. The contrast of devotion and treachery is striking. While the religious leaders conspire with Judas to plan Jesus' death, the woman, as an act of love and faith, prepares His body for burial.

Question 4. Before your group is too quick to agree with Jesus, note that the objectors raise legitimate concerns about the use of the perfume. You might want to divide your group in two and have them argue the merits of their particular position.

Questions 5–6. Some have thought Jesus' statement in verse 7 as uncompassionate toward the poor, but such a perspective loses sight that Jesus not only loved the poor, He was poor Himself. The woman recognizes that Jesus is the greatest of poor men. While the poor are "always" with them, this poor man would not "always" be present; He was about to die. It would be inappropriate to miss the opportunity. Jesus considers her act beautiful, worthy of remembrance because it recognizes the value of His death.

Questions 7–8. The Last Supper took place during the celebration of the Passover meal. During this meal families recalled the account of God's salvation of Israel from the tyranny of Egypt. The disciples could anticipate an evening of praise to God for His past provision and His future redemption. What the disciples did not fully anticipate was how the celebration of God's redemption would now focus on Jesus. These questions are meant to focus attention on the similarity and the difference between the Passover meal and the Communion meal.

Question 9. The woman's beautiful act took on much greater significance because it is linked with Jesus' death. The act both prepares Jesus' body for death and foreshadows His sacrifice as One who was to be "broken and poured out." You might also want to ask the group: *In what ways does the woman provide a model of acting on your convictions?*

Question 11. This question is meant to help the group focus on the meaning for us of Jesus' death. Encourage group members to be as specific as possible in their comments.

Question 12. As time permits, use this question as a summary to the entire twelve-study series. Feel free to go around the circle to allow each person to speak.

If each person in your group is a believer and comes from a church that permits informal communion services, a fitting closure would be to end your study with communion and prayer. It would be wise to check with your pastor or church leaders regarding this. In any event, focus on thanksgiving for the new ways you've gotten to know Jesus.

For Further Reading

Aharoni, Yohanan, and Michael Avi-Yonah, eds. *The MacMillan Bible Atlas*. Rev. ed. New York and London: Collier MacMillan Publishers, 1977.

Bonhoeffer, Dietrich. *The Cost of Discipleship*. New York: MacMillan, 1949.

Bruce, F.F., ed. *The New International Critical Commentary on the New Testament*. Grand Rapids: Eerdmans, 1986.

Douglas, J.D., F.F. Bruce, J.I. Packer, N. Hillyer, D. Guthrie, A.R. Millard, and D.J. Wiseman, eds. *New Bible Dictionary*. 2d ed. Leicester, England: Inter-Varsity Press, 1982.

Fee, Gordon, and Douglas Stuart. *How to Read the Bible for All It's Worth*. Grand Rapids: Zondervan, 1982.

Ferguson, Sinclair B. and David F. Wright, eds. *New Dictionary of Theology*. Downers Grove, Ill. and Leicester, England: InterVarsity Press, 1988.

Finzel, Hans. *Observe Interpret Apply: How to Study the Bible Inductively*. Wheaton, Ill.: Victor Books, 1994.

Fuller, Daniel. *Unity of the Bible*. Grand Rapids: Zondervan, 1992.

Gorman, Julie A. *Community That is Christian: A Handbook for Small Groups*. Wheaton, Ill.: Victor Books, 1993.

Green, Joel B., Scot McKnight, I. Howard Marshall. *Dictionary of Jesus and the Gospels*. Downers Grove, Ill.: InterVarsity Press, 1992.

Huggett, Joyce. *The Joy of Listening to God*. Downers Grove, Ill.: InterVarsity Press, 1987.

Kuhatschek, Jack. *Taking the Guesswork out of Applying the Bible*. Downers Grove, Ill.: InterVarsity Press, 1990.

Lewis, C.S. *Mere Christianity*. New York: MacMillan Publishing, 1960.

—————. *The Weight of Glory*. New York: MacMillan Publishing, 1980.

Piper, John. *Desiring God*. Portland, OR: Multnomah Press, 1986.

—————. *The Pleasures of God*. Portland, OR: Multnomah Press, 1991.

Plueddemann, Jim and Carol. *Pilgrims in Progress: Growing through Groups*. Wheaton, Ill.: Harold Shaw Publishers, 1990.

Stott, John R.W. *Basic Christianity*. Downers Grove, Ill.: Inter-Varsity Press, 1958.

—————. *The Cross of Christ*. Downers Grove, Ill.: InterVarsity Press, 1986.

Tasker, R.V.G., ed. *Tyndale New Testament Commentaries*. 20 vols. Grand Rapids: Eerdmans, 1963–1980.

Tenney, Merrill C., ed. *The Zondervan Pictorial Encyclopedia of the Bible*. 5 vols. Grand Rapids: Zondervan, 1975, 1976.

Walvoord, John F., and Roy B. Zuck, eds. *The Bible Knowledge Commentary, New Testament Edition*. Wheaton, Ill.: Victor Books, 1983.

Wenham, G.J., J.A. Motyer, D.A. Carson, and R.T. France, eds. *New Bible Commentary: 21st Century Edition*. Downers Grove, Ill. and Leicester, England: InterVarsity Press, 1994.

Wuthnow, Robert. *Sharing the Journey: Support Groups and America's New Quest for Community*. New York: The Free Press, 1994.

Author's Note: The resources on this list which have given me the most profound insight into knowing Jesus are John Piper's books *Desiring God* and *The Pleasures of God* along with Daniel Fuller's *Unity of the Bible*.

Notes and Prayers

About the Author

Bill Syrios spent his early years in Wooster, Ohio. Later with his parents, Bill and Barbara, sister Melinda and brother Jeff, he moved to Wichita, Kansas. There, the family came into contact with the *Jesus Movement* of the early 70s. It was within the local movement—called BASIC (Brothers and Sisters in Christ)—that knowing Jesus became a compelling life-endeavor for him.

Bill enrolled at *Emporia State University* where he found other like-minded friends in the campus group, *InterVarsity Christian Fellowship*. Besides getting a foundational experience in Christian community and a B.S.E. in history, Bill got something he didn't expect: a lifelong relationship with a woman.

Teresa and Bill married in June of 1976 and left Kansas for Pasadena, California. While Teresa drove the freeways and taught elementary school, Bill volunteered as an InterVarsity staff worker and graduated with an M. Div. from *Fuller Theological Seminary*. Upon moving to Portland, Oregon in 1980 (and later to Eugene in 1986), Bill served as an associate pastor in a Presbyterian church and as a staff member and area director with InterVarsity. Along the way they had four sons: Luke, Andrew, Phillip, and Mark.

In 1989 Bill started a real estate investment, construction, and management company, *Stewardship Properties*, in Eugene. Beside work, spending time with his family, and swimming for exercise, he is involved in helping to establish a new church, *River Oaks Community Church*. There Bill serves as a cell group facilitator and worship leader. Bill has published two previous Bible study guides: *Ecclesiastes* (with Teresa) and *Deciding Wisely*, both with InterVarsity Press.